THE INDESTRUCTIBLE HOUSEPLANT

TOVAH MARTIN

THE INDESTRUCTIBLE HOUSEPLANT

200 BEAUTIFUL PLANTS THAT EVERYONE CAN GROW

TIMBER PRESS
PORTLAND, OREGON

Copyright © 2015 by Tovah Martin. All rights reserved.
Published in 2015 by Timber Press, Inc.
Photographs copyright © 2015 by Kindra Clineff

The Haseltine Building
133 S.W. Second Avenue,
Suite 450
Portland, Oregon 97204-3527
timberpress.com

Printed in China
Cover design by Laken Wright
Original text design by Jeffrey Kurtz

Library of Congress Cataloging-in-Publication Data

Martin, Tovah, author.
  The indestructible houseplant : 200 beautiful plants that everyone
can grow/Tovah Martin ; photography by Kindra Clineff. — First edition.
    pages cm
  Includes bibliographical references and index.
  ISBN 978-1-60469-501-4
  1. House plants. I. Clineff, Kindra, photographer. II. Title.
SB419.M314 2015
635.9'65—dc23
                                                    2014042918

A catalog record for this book is also available from the British Library.

Frontispiece: Peperomias and a variegated
rubber plant (*Ficus elastica*) lounge in David
Whitman and Peter Stiglin's enclosed porch.

To my nephew and nieces—Ben Hutt, Hannah Hutt, and Emma Simmons—who will test the next generation of indestructibles

To Einstein, my research assistant

GROWING HOUSEPLANTS IN AN IMPERFECT, TIME-CHALLENGED WORLD 8

GALLERY OF INDESTRUCTIBLES 36

THE DETAILS 238

GROWING HOUSEPLANTS IN AN IMPERFECT, TIME-CHALLENGED WORLD

And here I thought I was all alone. I had no idea you were into houseplants too. All these years I've been quietly hoarding my houseful of plants without the faintest idea that, if given half a chance, you would be right alongside me growing up a storm in your windowsills. Like me, you crave green. With the same fervor, you would crowd every surface in your life with plants. You lust after wending vines tickling your legs as you bustle around the house. You share my passion for lush and verdant. You have always wanted an intimate relationship with something that photosynthesizes.

This book is for all the windowsill-gardener wannabes. When I realized how many of you are out there, and when I fielded the umpteenth request to recommend plants that would survive tough love, I knew what my next assignment was. For all the folks who hankered for houseplants but didn't know where to start, and for all the people who picked up the wrong houseplant and thought its hasty demise was their fault, this book is for you. We are going to make houseplants happen, and your life is going to be transformed.

Previous spread: Aloes and air plants are cool with colanders.

We all need nature. Many of us take every possible opportunity to slip outside. I have one foot out the door with the least provocation. But for half the year, going outside is difficult because I dwell in New England, where it can be truly dreadful on the far side of the front door. Beyond the awful interlude, for a couple of months leading in and out of what's officially marked on the calendar as the dormant season, it is mildly painful outside. So I focus inward. With a little peperomia stationed nearby and maybe an aspidistra or two within reach, I get my daily dose of nature.

Just like the scenes I see outdoors, my plants are exquisite. They work with my interiorscape, they feed into the ambiance, and they bring each room to another level. I don't have to devote a lot of time to the endeavor. My schedule looks a lot like yours and my to-do list needs to go on a diet, so I want a whole lot of green with minimal time investment.

There's never enough time. No matter what you do for a living or how many dependents are living in your home, both human and otherwise, the twenty-four-hour day doesn't begin to cover what you need to accomplish. You stretch the spare moments as far as they can go. But nobody can indulge in a high-maintenance hobby, even if it is going to make your life into nirvana, lower your blood pressure, transform your home office into a park, and give you something to blog about. As much as you share my passion for plants—and even though you agree that even one little houseplant is going to make the difference between a lifeless interior and a perky, uplifting, feel-good kind of place for the entire family (pets included)—nobody can afford to invest a glutton's share of the day in fussing over plants. The biggest stumbling block toward becoming a certifiable houseplant geek is lack of time. No matter how much I wedge houseplant upkeep into a few precious minutes each week, chore reduction is key. I need low maintenance, and so do you.

But most of us share another commonality. We are saddled with less-than-ideal growing conditions. I truly wish my home received more light. Most of my sills do not face south. I have only three windows that bask in bright light. These are jammed full of plants—it's standing room only, with a waiting list. Plus, my small lean-to greenhouse faces east, with obstructions on both sides (please note: I didn't build it). I have to curb my appetite for sun-loving plants. Most of the plants-in-residence are limited to individuals who do not gorge on sunrays. Indeed, most of my plants do perfectly well with extremely limited light. Even the succulents are just fine without a lot of wattage. Nothing is worse than watching a plant get spindly, stretch, and beg for more sunbeams, so I host plants that perform well on a strict low-lumen diet.

My house has all the typical impediments: no time, low light, an environment that vacillates between chilly and stuffy, and a Maine coon cat who loves to watch a plant plummet to the floor (more about Einstein later). And I hate to see a plant struggle, so I go with the toughies. There are no fussbudgets here. By the same token, plants that are prone to insect infestations need not apply. Plants that must loll in toasty temperatures would be doomed. I bet you have the same set of restrictions barring troublemakers from your happy home.

Einstein snuggled into a potted variegated tricyrtis (a perennial from outdoors that tolerates all sorts of abuse inside—including Einstein compression).

The good news is that after you winnow out all the needy, querulous, and persnickety candidates, there are still plenty of players left on the field. And, even better, they are readily available. You won't have to dig deep into the Sources section at the back of this book to track them down (but please do check out my favorite haunts). You can likely find these plants right in your neighborhood. You might even encounter some adorable adoptees in your local supermarket or big-box store. They probably have been neglected for a while, and they likely haven't seen the light of day for weeks before you wheeled them into the checkout line. But they look fine. Let that be a testimony to their fortitude.

No one needs to live without houseplants. This book is designed to enable you to invite plants into your inner sanctum so nature can work its magic for you and your family. Green tuffets of moss will pick up the texture of the sofa upholstery. Graceful lacy fern fronds will play opposites against a sleek marble table. From now on, coming home is going to be like taking a walk in the park. Your kitchen windowsill is going to be a garden. Life will be beautiful.

I'm nuts about houseplants—always have been.

WHERE I'M COMING FROM

Who am I to talk about houseplants? In a word, I'm an addict. My home is jammed with more plant life than is decently appropriate. We're not referring to a token houseplant or two. This is the gardening version of extreme sports. People brace themselves when they walk through my door and brush past the tangle of greenery. I wouldn't really call it a barrage, and hopefully nobody feels ambushed. But if you have one ounce of agoraphobic blood running through your veins, go elsewhere.

I have lots of houseplants under my belt. I've seen it all in the green department—the good, the bad, and the seductress. When you tell me your gardenia croaked, I know just where you're coming from. I don't expect you to embrace houseplants with a fetish similar to mine (however, if you do go overboard, welcome to the club). But I can confidently steer you toward plants that will give you positive feedback, especially if you are just testing the waters. I was amazed at how many plants stepped up to the plate while I was working on this book. The table of contents just kept getting longer.

And I face most of the same obstacles that trip you up. Although I have plenty of experience, I also face handicaps in my home. That's how I honed my repertory down to survivors. There are so many plants in my collection that some inevitably fall between the cracks.

Plants have been part of the picture here from the get-go. When I bought the house, the number of bathrooms wasn't really the deciding factor. Instead, I tallied up the number of windows. Houseplants have been members of my family from the earliest rustlings of my inner nature child. I spent twenty-five years at Logee's Greenhouses, a retail nursery that specializes in tropical plants. I was curator for the begonia

Ficus deltoidea makes a little forest together with a potted conifer in the converted barn.

A little scene of false aralia is stationed near the bookshelves.

collection, and spent stints tending the pelargoniums (otherwise known as zonal geraniums), herbs, succulents, and various other tropicals. I got lots of exposure early in my career. But when I moved on to western Connecticut, it didn't take long to get up to speed. The windowsills were filled to brimming before I finished unpacking the moving boxes.

Nearly two decades later, I still have some of those plants. But they did not all survive the shift, and that was an eye-opener. Many were not sufficiently durable to tolerate my level of tough love. I've run a lot of plants through endurance tests, and many victims fell by the wayside for one reason or another. You won't find the casualties in this book.

I live in a tiny town in a converted barn attached to an eighteenth-century cobbler shop (the oldest standing commercial building in town) via a lean-to greenhouse corridor with glass facing east. Although I surveyed the scene with an eye toward its potential for houseplants, not all of the indoor spaces turned out to be ideal hosts. For example, although my converted cow barn certainly has plenty of space as well as a bank of French doors, the incoming light is not bright. (The milkers were apparently more interested in chewing their cud than contemplating the scenery outside.) The other windows are relatively small. Thanks to the French doors, it's fairly bright in summer, but not during the rest of the year. That's bad news for flowering plants that make bright-light-or bust demands, but I've gravitated away from those specimens. The barn is where I conduct my most comprehensive houseplant-toughness testing. Only the brave come out alive.

The converted barn consists of a great room where I have my one piece of comfortable upholstery and a whole lot of hard surfaces with pillows in a feeble attempt to make them cozy. The interior décor was part of a conscious decision to keep the space plant-friendly. Most of the furniture is made of teak or other surfaces that won't be ruined if I set down a plant fitted with a saucer.

True to its name, the great room is a large, yawning space. It echoes without all of its furniture and plants. It could seem stark, but the plants take care of that. There is a lot of empty air above. I put in a few ladders, floor lamps, and vertical design elements so visitors send their eye upward rather than focus solely on what's at their elbows. But tall, linear plants also serve that function. Many plants in this book find life just ducky pulled away from the windows and stationed in the body of the room. Svelte indestructibles like ZZ plants, aspidistras, and bromeliads fill that space with their sinuous architectural physiques. I also have a dining table surrounded by mismatched swivel desk chairs and a huge bank of bookcases holding—you guessed it—a litany of horticultural titles.

On the other side of the bookcases is the kitchen. That's where the few and frugal barn windows let west-facing light come streaming in, which is a blessing in winter. They support small plants on the sills as well as more sizable plants on the tables that are stationed in front. These plants provide companionship while I prepare salads, dish out yogurt, and spoon this-or-that onto Einstein's plate while he weaves around my feet. When meal prep gets frantic and the salad greens start flying, the plants occasionally take a topple, which is stressful for everyone. But because they are in eyeshot while I'm waiting for the kale to boil, they receive more visits with the watering can than plants in further reaches of the house.

Then there is the cobbler shop. It was built in 1790, and in 1979 was converted into living space. It is a funky little building with wide, tall windows facing every exposure. All these windows hold houseplants, except those in my office. The office faces west, but

A group of bromeliads (members of the pineapple family), including *Tillandsia xerographica*, *Vriesea fenestralis*, and *Quesnelia marmorata*, sits in front of the French doors.

it is shaded by a generous porch overhang. Einstein spends most of his time here, either sleeping on my printer or monitoring the finches building their nests on the porch. The cat is a fellow houseplant aficionado, but with motives completely different from my own. Plants are his playmates. He does the stress and bounce testing, but he ingests only the cat grass grown for him. Many of the plants in this book are toxic to pets. This issue is addressed in The Details.

Einstein needs ample space to stretch out his rather lengthy frame after making things go bang in the night, and my office houses many of his beds. The room also holds the usual raft of machines, gadgets, and paper piles. Little space is left for plants, so only a few favorites are by my side. It is just as well, because if more of them were nearby, I would forever be hopping up to prune and water.

The menagerie in the bathroom is always changing because the plants love the spa treatment. Pictured are a selaginella moss, rhizomatous begonia, haworthia, and plectranthus.

Other windows in the cobbler shop are densely packed. The bathroom hosts loads of plants perched on half-round tiered plant stands that most people relegate to outdoors. One of my favorite indoor sports is shuffling plants on those stands, combining textures so they complement one another and bouncing color themes around. The room is spa treatment for plants. Ferns, begonias, mosses, and orchids go there for warmer and more humid conditions than the rest of the house can provide.

The upstairs windows are chilly, but large and filled with plants. My bedroom is bursting with plants. Einstein has to wedge between a Wardian case, a footed fern, and a hoya to sit on his pedestal and eye the deer dancing in the backyard. The room is tiny and furnished all in white, with a birch bark dresser, white vintage linens, and a Victorian dressing gown hung on the wall. But the decor is not monochromatic white because green is everywhere, from the plant-filled cloche sitting on my twig bedside table to the fronds stationed by the window. The plants awaken the room and make it cozy, romantic, and warm.

Between the two living spaces is the lean-to type greenhouse corridor, which has glass on the eastern exposure only. It is like a breezeway that joins together the cobbler shop and the converted barn. It is obstructed by the barn on one side and the cobbler shop on the other, and is shady most of the winter except for a sliver of light. Long custom-made bleachers line the glass side of the greenhouse in winter. In summer they go outside to give their plants an outdoor vacation, and I move some of the furniture from the barn into the space and sprinkle succulent plants around. Every morning I walk through the greenhouse corridor from my bedroom to the kitchen. Passing the plants is the highlight of my day. But even the greenhouse is less than perfect as a growing environment.

It's a nice try, but no hothouse princesses are permitted.

There are few absolutely ideal growing spaces in my house. So here I am, with an insatiable appetite for greenery and the same less-than-perfect situation you probably encounter. The solution is obvious: Go the durable route. And that's exactly what I do.

What's left are plenty of survivors. I'm such a plant geek that I don't stick solely with indestructibles. I grow plants of varying degrees of difficulty in my home. But to successfully cover every cranny with green, the ratio has to contain a very generous quantity of low-maintenance plants. If you do the math, count the hours in the day, and figure that I've got to earn a living, I can't fuss over individuals too much. You likely can't, either.

The plants in this book are tough. They love it when I bestow drinks with regularity and throw them a few words of encouragement. But when I have time only to admire them and blow them a kiss while rushing out the door, they don't pout. (Or, at least, it takes a while before they start to swoon.) And many can be resuscitated if things take a turn for the worse. Just when I think it's curtains for a kalanchoe, it pops back up from a seemingly dead stem.

But I don't push it. Sometimes a totally stressed plant will not come out of the twilight zone with its former good looks intact. I share with you, based on my experience, how to grow these plants so they shine. If your house is anything like mine—chilly, not sufficiently bright, cramped—they'll have plenty of challenges to surmount without adding more curveballs.

YOU AND YOUR HOME

I talk to you all the time. You call into radio shows where I am a guest, you come to my lectures, you post photos on my Facebook page. You tell me about your flaming Katy (*Kalanchoe blossfeldiana*), we touch base on your Christmas cactus (*Schlumbergera buckleyi*) and its timing, and we even discuss your spider plant (*Chlorophytum comosum*) and how to make it look presentable (relatively). We're almost family. Given my proclivity for houseplants, I bond with a lot of kindred spirits who cannot live without green. I have learned that no one has a perfect house for plants, and even fewer of us have the right situation in our offices. But that doesn't mean we are willing to go without.

You desperately want to succeed. You want that green scene in your home or office cubicle; you want nature by your side. And you want to do it beautifully. You will not settle for a perfunctory nod in the nature direction. You are dedicated to infusing your life with something poetic and meaningful. You want to play the perfect host. So we need to think about where, when, and how to make it happen.

The first step toward hosting houseplants is to find a space where they can reside. You need to fit plants into your existing living configuration. Start turning the pages and exploring the suggestions for plants that will suit all sorts of situations and tastes. I also show you how to design with plants that will work into your interior and lifestyle. This is going to be a happy marriage. But establishing a few parameters will make the relationship flow smoothly into happily ever after.

Everyone is different. Not only are our tastes divergent in plants, home styles, furniture, and just about everything else, but we also have varied growing conditions, talents, and issues. I tend to water sparsely, so succulents work like a charm for me. But you might be too liberal with the watering can. Some plants in this book won't mind if you pour on the water or withhold drinks; you could go either way with impunity. But others, like succulents, are custom made for those of us who water irregularly. And still others, like carex, are great for generous waterers. I tried to think of all types, and I took into account all sorts of growing conditions. If you have low light, I've got you covered. If you have a dry atmosphere, plants are included. If you need something tiny because of lack of space, you will find suggestions.

Start with a checklist of your conditions. All plants need light, and some require more than others. Begin your assessment by considering the sort of light situations you can offer. Are your windows large or small? What exposure do they face? South-facing windows tend to be bright, but not if they are obstructed by trees or other buildings. Most of the plants in this book do not require a sunny south-facing window, but many will enjoy it. (Those that cannot tolerate bright beams will be identified.) In winter, when growing houseplants becomes most critical, west-facing

A grouping of peperomias is sufficiently adaptable to go just about anywhere in your home or office.

If you need curtains, sheer might be the way to go for the sake of your rhipsalis.

windows offer very good light and can host all sorts of indestructible plants. Ditto for east-facing windows. Unless obstructed, those exposures are capable of furnishing sufficient light to host the bulk of the plants in this book. North-facing windows can be challenging for plants. Fortunately, some stoics such as aspidistras, ferns, ivies, sansevierias, ZZ plants, and several others tolerate very low light.

The type of curtains or blinds you use can affect the light available to your plants. The trend toward bulky window treatments puts houseplants at a disadvantage. If you need opaque curtains at night, consider installing them in a way that leaves maximum window space unobstructed during the day. Sheer curtains billowing in the breezes might be a good solution. They are romantic, handsome, and houseplant friendly. In my home, many windows go naked without any sort of treatments.

I don't use artificial lights for growing plants; I prefer the natural look in my home. However, it is a possibility, especially if you live or work where there is no light. But remember that this book discusses plants that will survive in challenging conditions. Try them in your space before you add electrical fixtures.

Be inventive when thinking about accommodating plants. Windowsills are just the beginning. Maybe you have limited sill space, or your sills are not sufficiently wide to balance plant containers. I enlist all types of furniture to get my plants close to the sunbeams. Plant stands are an obvious option, and they come in all shapes and sizes. I also employ tables of every description. Moist plants can leave marks on wood, so use glazed saucers to prevent leaks and tuck a cork coaster underneath. Although I have no really fine furniture in my house, I don't want to ruin the patina of chipped paint, so I have a variety of solutions, including placemats, plates, coasters, chargers, and zinc trays. I also corral a gamut of chairs, stools, stepladders, stacked vintage suitcases (remember when suitcases were rectangular and hard-sided?), wooden blocks, and everything else I can think of. Be creative. It's fun.

My house tends to be drafty (that's actually a gross understatement), but yours might be toasty. Either way, these plants are probably going to do just fine. They are selected on the basis of their fortitude when faced with Sahara-dry conditions. (Exceptions are identified.) Very warm temperatures blasting from heat sources such as woodstoves or forced hot air vents can lead to low humidity. That situation shouldn't be a problem with these plants. But if you want to increase humidity, you could use a humidifier or place plants together on a tray holding 1 inch (2.5 cm) of pebbles and ½ inch (1 cm) of water. Increasing the humidity in a home is good for preventing chapped lips, scaly skin, and cats that spark when you pet them. However, when you grow lots of plants, they increase humidity in the near vicinity of their brethren simply because they are huddled together with their moist soil. And a grouping of plants bears a wonderful resemblance to what happens outdoors. It reads as a slice from your hike in the woods or a snippet from your garden. On the other hand, misting is not an effective means of increasing humidity. You would need to do it almost constantly to make an impact, which could lead to fungal problems for your plant and fatigue for you. Skip it.

MEET THE
INDESTRUCTIBLES

Ask a nursery employee to point you toward low maintenance houseplants, and he or she will probably shrug and claim the entire inventory is indestructible. Sometimes the salesperson is eager to make a sale without any nasty reality checks. More often, he or she truly has no clue. The staff members have been blithely growing the plants for a few weeks, at most, under ideal conditions. What do they know about windowsills?

We know plenty about them. We know they can be drafty or stuffy. We wish our windowsills all basked in bright, unobstructed sunbeams, but our houseplants were not high on the architect's priority checklist. And even the best south-facing exposure gives light from only one angle. Plus, our cats are forever bogarting the sun. We know that houseplants are the victims of occasional bouts of forgetfulness and suffer from all the stresses incumbent in dry air, low light, and roving bugs looking for a square meal. But we scheme to wring every available square inch of space for its potential to host horticultural goodies. We milk the lumens for all they are worth. So we need the foot soldiers.

The plants in this book belong in the combat unit. Of course, there are different levels of ironclad represented, and they are classified as either Easy or Easiest. Some give less-than-ideal conditions a stiff upper lip and bumble along nonetheless, while others can be half-forgotten for long periods of time and still come out smiling. It's the difference between tough love and total neglect. Of course, I suggest lavishing love on everything. But we live in an imperfect world.

A little disclaimer here: There is no such thing as truly indestructible. If you try hard enough, you

Although her heart belongs to geraniums (see page 116), Lee Link hosts all descriptions of indestructibles in her home, including (clockwise from top) euphorbia, ivy, and aloe.

can destroy anything. If you put any of these plants through the paper shredder, leave them in the car with the windows closed, or locate them anywhere near my goats, they will indeed die. My talented nephew has managed to dispatch some of the plants in these pages to horticultural heaven. But with normal wear and tear in the average home or office, these plants are as rock solid as possible. Many require more effort to kill than to keep alive.

The plants in this book are worth growing. Everyone has personal likes and dislikes, but I am not suggesting the dregs of the plant kingdom for your windowsills. You want quality. You want entertainment. Beauty is what your home is all about. And I am right alongside you. All these plants are part of my green family. They pass the Tovah test, and I don't fall for any old green thing.

I have my prejudices, but I try to be liberal. I once declared no spider plants would be allowed through my entryway, but that was before I met *Chlorophytum comosum* 'Bonnie,' a curly-leaf version that I simply adore. Similarly, a few years ago, Chinese evergreens (*Aglaonema* species) were turned away by the bouncer at the door. But with the riveting new hybrids available, I welcome them in with VIP seating. Ditto for dracaenas.

This book may not represent every indestructible plant in the marketplace. When in doubt, do your own testing. But the plants in these pages tend to tolerate sub-par conditions and less-than-perfect gardeners. Some genera are famed for their fortitude, such as aloes, bromeliads, hoyas, and ivies. Other families have some sticky wickets in the clan but also claim an easygoing relative or two. Often, durable plants share certain physical traits. Many indestructibles have leathery, tough-skinned leaves rather than delicate foliage. But that isn't always the case. Nerve plants

(*Fittonia*) and beefsteak plants (*Iresine*) certainly don't look bulletproof, and yet they tolerate their fair share of abuse without a whimper. It would be nice if I could say, "Head right over to the plants with long, sword-like leaves in the nursery; they can take whatever insults you want to hand out." But it doesn't always work that way.

I wish more indestructibles produced bounteous flowers. Unfortunately, it seems that blossoms do not go hand in hand with tough skins. There are exceptions. If blooms are high on your wish list, head straight for a flaming Katy (*Kalanchoe blossfeldiana*) or medinilla. But try to see the full picture. Leaves can be pretty darn breathtaking. Consider the diversity of leaf colors, shapes, patterns, and textures that are presented here, and you might decide they compete favorably with flower power. It's exciting to boast that your moth orchid rebloomed. But how about growing a plant with thrills that never pause? Great foliage will do that for you.

The diversity of these plants actually works in your favor. You will find specimens of all descriptions in the indestructible category. You are bound to meet plenty of individuals that tug at your heartstrings. And you can work with plants to achieve whatever style works in your domain. One of my favorite challenges is to transform a plant I once classified as dowdy. At this point, I can make just about anything look like it belongs in the haute crowd. I just slap it into an old florist's vase or give it a milky white McCoy, and it is Cinderella.

You might wonder where I obtained the plants in these pages. I have an insatiable appetite for plants, but no time. I rarely have the opportunity to go to specialty nurseries, so most of my plants come from local mom-and-pop stores that neither give them the royal treatment nor have a wonderfully broad and exciting inventory. Indeed, many of my adoptees come from a

Ironclad plants tend to have thick leaves, like these members of the prayer plant group sitting beside a rhizomatous begonia in my bathroom.

nearby horticultural therapy facility. And you wouldn't believe how many of the plants in this book were purchased at supermarkets and big-box stores. I even drag plants home from yard sales. Taking in a plant in need is part of the fun. Einstein originally came from a shelter too. Adoption feels good.

Maybe I was a plant snob once upon a time, but no longer. The moment I moved into a house with less-than-ideal growing conditions, I quickly lost any vestige of a plant attitude. I hope you will see the silver lining in dolling up any plant.

TRIED AND FAILED

I ran lots of plants through their paces while working on this book. I started with those that were generally billed as diehards. I marched them up and down the stress tests (Einstein helped), and most succeeded with flying colors. Those that did not were bumped from the toughie list. Several ficus were failures, and other surprises bit the dust.

I've often seen flowering maples (*Abutilon* cultivars) billed as a piece of cake. A flowering maple has leaves that resemble what's on the standard Canadian flag, as well as mallow-like blossoms. In the best of all worlds, they would bloom throughout the year. But they do not really perform except in summer. Even worse, they drop leaves in winter, which can be depressing, especially if you had hoped to host something that looks alive. In addition, flowering maples love to play host to a long list of insects. You don't need this headache.

I was planning to profile strawberry begonia (*Saxifraga stolonifera*). It has roundish dark green leaves with silver veins (like a begonia) that form rosettes and send out runners with plantlets attached (like a strawberry). In spring, candelabra-like stems of little white flowers pop up. It's adorable, and I've seen plants in supermarkets just begging to come home with me. I tried to play host, but my strawberry begonia kept coming down with powdery mildew. I thought it was the weather or possibly my ineptitude, so I removed the offending parts and tried again with one of the runners. Aphids attacked its flower stalks. I scratched this plant from the indestructible list.

Oh, how I'd love to have a citrus orchard indoors. Some advertisements make it sound like child's play. Well, citrus are a challenge. I stumble along with a Calamondin orange (*Citrofortunella microcarpa*) and keep nudging it to produce those heavenly fragrant flowers followed by a crop of juicy fruit. But it always looks a little peaked. In fact, it's a little bit of an embarrassment, with yellowish leaves in winter. Calamondin orange is one of the easier citrus to grow. These plants need almost constant fertilizer. They are definitely not in the indestructible domain.

I can't say I'm dying to grow cacti. They're a little bit too thorny for my liking, and I don't have sufficient sun. Unless you have a very bright exposure, cacti might not be the plants for you, even though they rarely require water and need no interaction whatsoever. But then again, who wants to embrace a cactus?

I was hoping to include coleus (*Solenostemon* cultivars) in these pages. I brought some in before the first frost in autumn to serve as houseplants. We got off to a great start, but then the furnace kicked in and our relationship began to deteriorate rapidly. First my coleus was forever wilted. Then it came down with a malady I call the snivels, the main symptom being new growth that just melts away. Then came aphids and whitefly. Yuck. I tried again. Yuck, the sequel.

Hellebores are a delight to entertain in colder months. They start blooming right after the holidays and make life pretty swell throughout the winter. I wouldn't be without one. But hellebores are thirsty plants, and they don't respond well to deprivation, as wilting leads to fungal problems. If you're willing to put in the time, go for it. But I can't refer to them as indestructible.

I've seen a lot of elephant's ears (*Alocasia* cultivars) at big-box stores. I am so tempted. In fact, I succumbed this year, knowing full well they require warmer temperatures than I can furnish. And sure enough, the plant is slowly losing leaves and not gaining replacements. I haven't lost it yet, but it's definitely not a stalwart. It also needs high humidity. My house offers that part of the configuration, but high humidity is not usually coupled with warm temperatures—except in the tropics, where these plants are native.

I've lusted after arrowhead vine (aka goosefoot), *Syngonium podophyllum*. The arrow-shaped leaves come in some very tempting colors with pinks and reds in the center. And heaven knows, I tried. But the leaves always turn a sickly yellow color and slowly droop. I finally crossed it off the list.

I could go on. In fact, many of the families of plants in this book have one or two sticky wickets in their closets. In the begonia group, the colorfully leaved rex types are difficult. With the ferns, beware of the maidenhair and Boston fern types. With African violets, steer clear of the Cape primrose (*Streptocarpus*) group unless you have very warm temperatures. But I've identified these in each chapter. After you read this book, you may graduate into the expert realm. In that case, try more challenging plants—if you have the right conditions.

INDESTRUCTIBLES IN YOUR DECOR

Invincible can look like a million bucks. The photographs in this book show that indestructible does not mean dowdy. Of course, any plant can go either way. But if you put a little thought into designing with houseplants, they can make a scene sparkle. It doesn't take much to turn the tide into awesome. In fact, this is the fun part.

Consider your space and think about how a little nature might improve the atmosphere. Scientific tests have substantiated that plants benefit the air quality indoors. That in itself is a critical role for a green thing to play in your life. But houseplants also keep you linked to nature. They establish the bond with botany on a daily basis. When you live with something, the intimacy creates a deeper relationship beyond anything that is apt to happen when walls stand between you and nature. You interact with that plant, you see its glory, you smell its leaves and flowers, and you come to know it. You may laugh when I say that a geranium becomes family, but it's true.

Go into a room in your house, shuffle over to a blank space near a light source, and hold up one of the pictures in this book. Do you like it? Go one step further and incorporate the image into what you would like to see in your environment. Work with the wall colors, pick up the echo of a rug hue, or play off the curves of a lamp. Plants can do a lot for a room. At the very least, there's something about green that is both uplifting and calming. Every room in your house could offer that exhale opportunity. Substitute a plant for a knick-knack or two. Rather than dusting, you'll be visiting your plant occasionally with a watering can. Seems like a worthwhile trade-off.

A group of
bird's nest ferns
(*Asplenium
nidus*) combined
with one of my
other favorite
houseplants,
fiber optic grass
(*Isolepis cernua*),
forms a garden
indoors.

Whether your home is classic, vintage, or modern, plants merge into the space and serve a function. Plants will brighten a drab area, give any room a theme, and tie elements together as a cohesive fixture. They can also ease the tone to calm a space into restive. If walls are light, green plants reinforce the sense of summer. If walls are dark, plants serve as a beacon to brighten the surroundings. They contribute a textural dialogue with shiny surfaces or soften the stiffer lines of furniture. Plants also weave magic into office environments. Many companies have incorporated plants into their public areas. Go the next step and bring nature into your cubicle. Indestructible houseplants will not interfere with your workday routine or pout over weekends and vacations when you are elsewhere. They can be their own boss.

What does a room need to become a botanical host? A window helps. For many of the plants in this book, most windows will work. The more light a window introduces into the scene, the more your possibilities broaden. Plus, additional light improves the appearance of plants. Ivy in a poorly lit north window will probably not look as good as ivy given a slightly brighter exposure. Beyond that, it's merely a matter of positioning: Try to snuggle that plant close to the window, if possible, or within 36 inches (91 cm) of the light source. Put it on a shelf so the entire growing part of the plant soaks in light. I do a lot of coupling with ground covers, especially for plants with woody stems that leave plain brown soil exposed. That soil surface will also need some light, depending on what you're coupling. Position the plant so light falls on the edge of the container as well as the upper portions, if possible. The results will spell the difference between a spaceholder and a compliment gatherer.

That's the ideal, but in many cases it is not feasible to nestle a plant immediately in the direct pathway of

Peace lily (*Spathiphyllum*) is one of the best plants for cleaning air, and it can look very different depending on its presentation. Here it goes rustic.

Got a modern home? Peace lily can take on a contemporary spin.

My home is seriously retro, and peace lily works beautifully with the time-warped ambience.

a light source. Or maybe, like me, you host so many plants that not everyone can groove in the light. Or perhaps you want to bring plants into the midst of a room. With indestructibles, it's often possible to move away with impunity from the immediate area around a window. Try aspidistras, ferns, ficus, ivies, mosses, spathiphyllums, spider plants, and many of the other low-light plants in this book to increase the reach of green into the heart of your living space. If your goal is saturation coverage, indestructibles are your co-conspirators.

The first hurdle to surmount with houseplants is the initial turnoff. You go into a garden center and encounter a bunch of unhappy plants anchored pathetically in their plastic pots. No one could blame you for failing to feel a spark. They haven't been watered, they haven't been groomed, and they look like refugees. Nothing in that picture is going to seduce you into adoption.

But what if that forlorn plant could be made to look magnificent? What if you found just the right combination of container and setting to turn it around? Give anything the royal treatment and it shines. Even plants that might have evoked nothing more than a yawn will blossom, so to speak—it's the botanical version of stilettos or a tuxedo. Any plant can become a supermodel when you work up its finer points, and the whole room will be the lucky beneficiary. Houseplants have the potential to look like sculpture, a masterpiece, and a piece of art. However, your assistance is mandatory. This isn't somebody else's craftsmanship. You are the sculptor.

I've seen a lot of lackluster ZZ plants (*Zamioculcas zamiifolia*), but if you match one with a cool container, it gains a new sense of importance.

When you work with indestructible houseplants, you won't be struggling to keep your new family member alive and well. Instead, you can throw all your energy into the creative process. Pulling together the look begins the process. Play off the texture of an air plant set in a glass bowl or couple it with a carved wood receptacle. Place a philodendron with a slight maroon cast in a bright red bucket. Think about attributes in the plant that you could accentuate. Beyond color and texture, consider lines and form. This should be as much fun as flower arranging. After the initial pulling together and potting up, you can just sit back and bask. That's not to say you won't be spending endless hours admiring your creativity. Your work of art will likely inform all your waking hours and put a shine on your days and nights. The investment that you made in the beginning will pay off.

The more thought you put into the display, the more fulfilling the reward becomes, so be adventurous. Push the envelope with combinations that command attention. Go for a creative container that demands a second glance. But also consider making a meaningful vignette. Bring other elements into the picture. Play textures, colors, and themes together. You might work with natural elements: Maybe you have a tree stump table, a carved stone stool, a collection of seashells, or a bouquet of dried allium stalks. Or maybe you want to combine textiles, architectural salvage, grandfather clocks, telescopes, globes, and sundials. You are going to have a blast.

The lonesome little supermarket purchase you made on a whim has the potential for reaching high acclaim. It hardly seemed possible when you saw it on the way to the Valencia oranges. But the moment you adopt it, the whole script changes.

WORK IT

How you showcase a plant is everything. Plants are not necessarily at the height of their career when they come home with me. I've trawled the big-box florist department and accepted castoff plants from friends. Any plant can get a makeover, no matter how ordinary it might be. If you give that flea market discard a throne, it is going to reign.

The container is a good start toward glam. That relationship begins the chemistry bubbling. You owe it to the plant, yourself, your home, and your family (not necessarily in that order) to get your newly adopted green thing out of its original plastic pot as quickly as possible. Initiate the beauty treatments immediately, before you lose interest. Repot into something wonderful.

Your first considerations should be practical. You want something cool, but you also need a container that works for your plant. Start by checking the root system. Pull the plant out of its original container and examine the roots to see if they have filled the pot. If not, your target container should be the same size or even smaller than the original pot. If you see a network of white, healthy roots, consider giving that plant a slight promotion. I suggest no more than a 2-inch (5 cm) graduation at a time so your plant does not swim in a gigantic frame. It's like shoe sizes—you don't want to get blisters.

Once you've figured out the general size of a target container, you can have a field day. When I lecture, the most commonly asked question is, "Where do you get your containers?" The answer is, "Everywhere." I drag containers home from wherever I roam. You just can't imagine how many pots have gone through airport security (successfully, I might add). I am forever haunting garden centers, and there is an impressive

Indestructibles let you have a lark, like this athyrium fern in a funnel.

array of containers available in the mainstream nowadays. I prefer to work with terra-cotta, cement, or metal for a natural look. Glazing is fine and can add a fun spin when playing off a color in a flower or foliage. I like matching moods in a room, and my house is decidedly yesteryear. Who doesn't love a crackle finish? You can find containers with all sorts of glazes (see the Sources section for some of my favorite vendors).

Be sure to look for drainage holes, especially if the container is so expensive that you might not want to drill. It sounds obvious, but drainage isn't a given. Some manufacturers don't understand that plants need an outlet for excess water to escape. Other makers imagine their containers will be used as cachepots. I prefer to plant directly in a pot rather than use it as a receptacle for a plastic container. I believe plants grow better in a breathable base than in plastic, but that's my prejudice. Go your own way.

Feel free to explore beyond sanctioned containers. I use just about anything I can enlist, including buckets, industrial cylinders, kitchen pots and pans, and strainers. I get hollowed tree stumps and faux bois items. I drill a lot of holes, using a cement bit for metal and a masonry bit for terra-cotta. I never sidestep practicality. I grow in colanders, but I use succulents that love drying out, and I put them on zinc trays so the water seeping from all those drainage holes has somewhere to escape and does not ruin the furniture.

Select shapes according to your taste, but remember that a container's silhouette should be firmly based in practical considerations. Real estate is tight near my light sources, so I gravitate toward long, thin cylinder shapes rather than broad footprints. There are exceptions: Begonia and bromeliad roots tend to spread horizontally rather than plunge downward, so I give them shallow, squat pots. And I shy away from bean pot–shaped containers because they are a hassle to repot. (When you have a container with a smaller mouth cinching in from a wider belly, it is a struggle to free the root system.) For aesthetic purposes, I dote on containers with sleek lines. But I've learned the hard way that containers with a very broad mouth tapering into a tiny base are prone to jumping off the windowsill. When I find them smashed into bits on the floor, Einstein assures me he had nothing to do with their suicidal tendencies.

Saucers are essential. Many indoor gardeners imagine they will skip saucers and simply bring their plants to the sink whenever they need a drink. That's just asking for failure. Once you make a plant high maintenance, it's doomed. Add beautiful saucers into the creative dialogue. Don't resort to clear plastic versions that do no justice to your gorgeous work of art. Plates are one of my favorite money-saving tricks. In fact, I'm running out of plates for the dining room table. Take care not to put a saucer on wood without a cork coaster or something similar underneath to avoid leaving stains or mildew marks. I often work with zinc baking trays beneath a little colony of potted plants.

Now expand the picture to include some furniture. As you thumb through these pages, you'll discover that my house is glaringly devoid of expensive furniture. Most of my tables are flea market finds or antique shop acquisitions. I use everything and anything as a plant stand. I have a few sanctioned stands, but they often hold only a single plant, which doesn't go far for an addict of my proportions. I've enlisted every type of table imaginable for the purpose (my favorite is a demilune), as well as anything I can stack up (such as vintage suitcases) or otherwise convince to shoulder a plant. Outdoor furniture comes in during the winter for plant-cradling purposes. I try to be inventive. I've even been known to balance one table on another to raise it up to window height. For Einstein, all these

A tall stand with room only for one plant on its top is pretty much Einstein-proof.

contrivances are like a jungle gym. He just loves leaping from one table to the next and checking out the window views from each vantage point—to the peril of all the plants on board, of course. I station particularly pet-toxic plants on tall, slender plant stands that he cannot access. I discuss plant toxicity in the back of the book, and many of the plants in this book are indeed poisonous. Because it's safest to assume that all houseplants are inedible, and because toxicity is a complex issue, I mention toxicity only in the sidebars of houseplants the ASPCA identifies as "most toxic to pets." But please, keep critters (and the flying circuses in their wake) in mind when you pull your scenes together.

If you build out from there, adding more stools, plant stands, and whatnot, you'll be amazed at how many plants a window can support. Be careful not to obstruct the incoming beams with tall or bulky plants close to the panes. Pretty soon you'll have a garden inside, and that's just what you had in mind.

A chorus line of flowering kale is amazingly low maintenance indoors.

COMBINING UNKILLABLES

Just you wait: When greenery begins taking over your life and your successes start mounting, the momentum will lead deeper into green. You are bound to want more.

The beauty of green invincibles is that they make good company. When individuals are not prima donnas, they tend to mingle well with compatriots. You've probably noticed the same phenomenon in your workplace and social life. Would you rather work with the high-maintenance types or the foot soldiers? I thought so.

These plants lend themselves to mixing and matching. Throughout this book, each profile mentions other plants that can grow in unison. They can all coexist clustered happily together. Growing houseplants is a lot like gardening outdoors, so you can create scenes by playing plants off each other with complementary or matching colors, textures, and shapes. Working with indestructibles makes it particularly easy to consult your inner artist. With a never-say-die team, you can become a garden designer indoors. I can't tell you how much fun it is to create vignettes.

But this goes beyond merely setting simpatico plants side by side. You can create mini landscapes (I call them windowscapes) indoors. Use a container to make a little garden using all the theories and practices you would employ on a much larger scale outdoors. Work a scene of peperomias with different physical traits in a metal baker's pan or wooden trade box. One might look like a mini tree, while another will be the ground cover sprawling at its feet. Still another might form tufts to fill in the midrange space. The end result will look like someone shrank the perennial bed and put it on your windowsill. It's a terrarium-like scene, minus the glass.

Rock-solid
kalanchoes work
as a team in a
colander, and
they all love
the additional
drainage.

This practice works well with indestructibles because they are so easygoing. They are made for relationships. But the secret to success lies in selecting plants with similar needs. Succulents are wonderful playmates, but these bright light worshippers don't romp well with the darker personalities of ferns and mosses. Another detail to consider is growth habit. Two very energetic ground covers in a container might play fisticuffs. But if you pair an athletic ground cover with a slow-growing plant that shoots up vertically, you've pulled together a great marriage and brought your indestructibles to the next level. More detailed instructions can be found in the Mixing and Matching section, but it's never too soon to start thinking about the possibilities for entertaining plants and nature together.

You can also add nongrowing items to the brew. I like to bring other elements of nature into my scenes. I build up mini terrains by using rocks that I have found in my travels. I put in seashells, fossils, driftwood, seedpods, and lichen-covered sticks, and I use faux bird's nests, twigs, and other finds. Sometimes I even tuck in shards from broken pots and other shattered bits from tiles and pottery. Because I live in a farming community, I can find plenty of vintage glass electrical insulators and that sort of thing, and I put them to use. One year my garden statue of Pan broke, so I tucked what remained into the base of a plant and called it "Fractured Fairytales."

A mixed container is one idea, or you could group together individually potted plants into a little village by the window. Love the forest? Find a hollow log and plant it with ferns beside some Norfolk Island pines planted in faux tree bark containers. Adore the beach? Line up some bromeliads with seashells displayed in between. Miss the garden? When nurseries are staging their autumn sales, grab some flowering kales for a song, pop them into a window box, and watch them erupt into flowers. (This particular masterpiece won't last forever, but it will be golden for a few months in fall.)

The beauty of working with invincibles is that whatever you do, it is no sweat. No matter how you design with your indestructibles, whether coupling them together in vignettes that work in tandem or tucking them all into a communal container, your job is simple because you are dealing with an easy-to-please crowd.

This hollowed-out log is actually a planter with drainage holes and a cavity to receive the moss and ferns that dwell in peace and harmony within.

GALLERY OF INDESTRUCTIBLES

This book presents house-plants that have withstood the tests. They have been ignored. When the watering can was making the rounds, it occasionally failed to tarry over their dry soil. Some have even wilted. In many cases, these gallant plants have stood back, giving the prime spots in the sunbeams to needier green companions. Occasionally they have been relegated to north windows and equally unpropitious locations. But there is no need to feel sorry for these guys; they are the botanical versions of the Marines.

I define an indestructible plant by its ability to bounce back from punches. I did not focus only on plants that can tolerate low light or lack of water. Homes have all sorts of situations available, and some are bright and some are not so well lit. There are also all types of indoor gardeners. Some water sporadically, while others cannot hold back from applying the spout often and sometimes obsessively.

Most important, these plants are beautiful. This criterion is where a lot of plants fell out of the running. I avoided spaceholders. If a plant is just stuffed into a corner, it is not going to further the cause of bonding you with nature. I selected memorable plants that would not be forgotten, and suggest displays that will up their profile so they glow. You won't see any slackers here, and every individual should make you yearn to cohabitate with it more closely.

Along the way, I noticed that lots of my friends are thinking likewise, so we took some field trips to other homes with cutting-edge but unkillable collections. Most of my pals are somehow linked with gardening,

but they're also wildly busy. They are antique dealers, shopkeepers, architects, caterers, and artists. They have absolutely no time to spend fussing. But I stepped into their domains and found incredibly comely plants sharing their homes and lifestyles. I showcase some of their talent, creativity, successes, knowledge, and brilliance in the stories sprinkled throughout this book, and I hope they further inspire and nudge you to try indoor gardening with all your creative juices flowing. My friends are living proof that anyone can do it—with impressive panache. Please join us.

Aloes make great bedfellows, and they are so easy to accommodate. You can even tuck them into a colander.

Previous spread: Peperomias in wood-clad containers serve as a centerpiece on David Whitman and Peter Stiglin's table.

AFRICAN VIOLET

Because they remain diminutive, stashing African violets (*Saintpaulia* cultivars) in cement cubes and zinc pots works great, especially if they can soak up water from below.

Let the rehab begin. Long ago, I decided it was time to blow off the cobwebs and give old faithfuls a second coming, and I encourage you to do likewise. Many of the plants in this book could use a dusting off. You know them way back when, and you are prone to dismiss them as part of the murky past, like bell bottoms and fondue. But wait. Not all the plants from your far-out youth deserve to fall into the has-been category. Give them an updated role.

If ever a plant needed to move into the here and now, it is the African violet. It is so strongly linked with doilies and tea parties that many indoor gardeners figure it doesn't have a future. But these plants survived indoor gardening's dark ages intact, which is a huge recommendation for their reliability. African violets could be called the golden retrievers of indoor gardening. They aim to please. Give them a chance to prove themselves yet again.

The African violet fraternity has a long reach. Within the Gesneriad family, all sorts of relations have been enlisted indoors. I zero in on the real diehards, African violets (*Saintpaulia ionantha* cultivars) and *Chirita* cultivars. These are the most durable of the clan, and I've done the litmus tests to prove it. My chilly house cannot host most gesneriads in a manner that pleases their toasty hearts. Cape primrose (*Streptocarpus*) does not even put up a struggle; it just perishes. Similarly, columneas, aeschynanthus, and most of the other members of this family give my cool home the cold shoulder. I haven't even tried miniature sinningias because I know they're doomed. But African violets and chiritas are a different story. They love me.

Everyone can picture the little rosette of soil-hugging felted leaves clustered around a bouquet of violet look-alike flowers. African violets can endure lack of humidity, lapses in watering, and low light, and still live to tell the tale. But beyond mere survival, they blithely blossom their way through hell (from a houseplant's point of view—nothing against your home). You cannot dissuade an African violet from blooming. It just wants to pump out those flowers. Yes, its leaves and blossoms will become mottled if you splash cold water on them. Yes, those same leaves might wrinkle up slightly beside a chilly window. But the flowers keep coming.

The botanical world has done a lot with African violet flowers recently. At flower shows, the blossoms look like someone pumped them full of steroids. They are ruffled. They are all shades of colors (mostly in the pink and purple realm). They are splashed and flecked with different hues. And they are immense. But you know what? Call me a purist, but I prefer the simple single flowers that are a dead ringer for hardy violets in the garden. Ditto for the foliage. Give me the plain, swank dark leaves rather than variegated versions any day.

How can you reinvent these plants that have so much baggage? Easy. Give them the sleekest presentation you can pull together. I put mine in thoroughly modern containers

Chirita 'Aiko' expands the color range of African violets into glowing yellow, and it blossoms continually.

The blossoms of
Chirita 'Aiko' read
from a distance.

for a face-lift. I go for glazed terra-cotta with stripes or zigzags or chic metal, and then I create a vignette around it. Singly displayed, African violets are never going to be the sort of plant you can notice from across the room. But cluster a few together and you've got the volume a chorus can create. I saw a retrospective-chic display at the Chicago Flower Show of six African violets tucked into an old leather satchel, and it was mighty cool. You could do the same thing with a picnic basket, although you might want to tuck a zinc tray within so you can water from below. Add some spike moss and you're cooking.

If you don't splash water, African violets shouldn't require the white-glove treatment of water from below only. I've grown plenty and watered them conventionally without suffering consequences. But I wait for the water to warm up before applying it in winter. And I take aim with the watering can to direct the stream away from the leaves. (This is easy enough if you're paying attention.) Note that African violets don't fare very well in cold rain outdoors. In fact, you might as well keep them inside during the warm season. They don't appreciate summer camp.

Temperature-wise, I push it. African violets would prefer nothing lower than 60°F (15°C) at night with a 5- to 10-degree jump during the day, but it's not going to happen in my house in autumn, winter, and early spring. They chug along nonetheless. I don't give them special African violet potting soil, although they would love it. Instead, I sink the roots in my usual organic potting soil, taking care to give them just enough room to feel cozy but not swim. I water them when the soil is slightly dry but not parched. Overwatering is a killer.

I treat my chiritas the same way. Chiritas resemble African violets, but they have tubular blossoms. I thought pinks and baby blues were the extent of their color range until I met *Chirita* 'Aiko' (*C. eburnea* × *C. subrhomboidea*), which has primrose yellow blossoms on foot-long spires above a rosette of long tongue-like leaves. I love it. It hasn't stopped blooming throughout autumn and winter. But all chiritas perform for me. I haven't found a bad egg in the bunch. They send up flower spike after flower spike even when I forget to water. Their leaves can mottle if you splash them with cold water, but it usually doesn't mar the plant over the long run. And chirita leaves are occasionally silver flecked and generally look good. Some chiritas become lanky and sprawling with time. If this happens, prune them back and root the cuttings. The mother plant will regrow to hug the soil and look tidy again.

Chirita 'Aiko' has sufficient presence to make a statement from a distance. But most chiritas are about the same size as African violets and could be displayed in similar vignettes. They are great neighbors for begonias, especially because blue is not in the begonia color spectrum for flowers, so they add another element. And, of course, chiritas are wonderful beside African violets. Just don't do doilies. That's all I ask.

AFRICAN VIOLET
Saintpaulia and *Chirita*
EASY

SIZE	Usually less than 4 inches (10 cm) high
FOLIAGE	Frequently felted and good-looking; generally forming rosettes
OTHER ATTRIBUTES	Adorable, colorful blossoms
EXPOSURE	East or west
WATER REQUIREMENTS	Allow soil to dry out between waterings; do not wet leaves
OPTIMUM NIGHTTIME TEMPERATURE	60–65°F (15–18°C)
RATE OF GROWTH	Slow to medium
SOIL TYPE	Rich, humusy, peaty potting soil with compost included
FERTILIZING	Early spring to late autumn
ISSUES	Foliage can become marred if cold water falls on the leaves
COMPANIONS	Begonias, bromeliads, ferns, mosses, nerve plants, and prayer plants

AGAVE

Agave parryi brandishes barbs, but it's not as bad as some of its kin. It almost never needs water in this cylinder.

In general, I'm a softy. My tastes run more toward fluffy and cuddly than spiky things (Einstein being a good example). I'm attracted to touchables as opposed to tough love. But I'm not just a hands-on type of person with a penchant for reaching out and petting things. I'm also a clod, a fumbler. What's more, I'm a fast-moving klutz. I've learned not to run with scissors. But another survival tactic has to do with avoiding roommates that brandish sharp weapons. That's why I've limited the number of agaves in residence.

I wish it could be otherwise. Every year I go to various plant sales (Trade Secrets in Sharon, Connecticut, is a favorite) and lust after an agave or two. When making a statement, nothing compares. You walk into a room, you see an agave (you can't miss it), and you are struck by its sleek physique. It has that sort of startling vavoom that serves as an exclamation point without further ado. Not only does it say plenty in a small space, but you feel the power of that take-no-prisoners plant. Agaves are a strong presence, and I would love to fill my life with them, except that I also have the certain knowledge that if there were a whole lot of agaves in my life, I would eventually get pierced— probably in the eye.

Fortunately, some crannies of my home are low-traffic areas. I don't come in contact with these alcoves on a regular basis. And viewing an agave from a respectful distance is definitely the way to go. The converted barn is vast and yawning with a bank of French doors facing east, so it offers plenty of infrequently traveled opportunities to host plants. It is sufficiently spacious to allow me to grow a few agaves and other toothy plants that pack potential bite. And because the comfy furniture is clustered away from those areas, I can safely entertain guests without issuing scratch-and-dent warnings. Other people put up gates for snarling dogs; I keep nippy succulents segregated from innocent passersby. The last thing you want is for your agave to reach out and touch someone.

It is a testimony to the fortitude of agaves that they can survive in the recesses of my converted barn. I designed the French doors to have a full bank of windows, but in midwinter, the east-facing panes do not gather significant sun. Instead, the light seems to be filtered into ambient brightness rather than full beams. The diminishing glimmer is even more pronounced further from the light source. As a result, I found the perfect place to position an agave where it would command center stage for its architectural splendor but remain clear of foot traffic. Since they are succulents, I initially feared the agaves would slowly fade away if given minimal light. But an agave in low light performs pretty much the same as an agave given full front-row sunbeams.

I suspect the less-than-ideal positioning has hindered my agave from blooming. But that might be a good thing, as the rosette from which the flower stalk pokes is doomed to perish not long after the flower show comes and goes. It is one of nature's tragedies, for sure, but a flower is an agave's last hurrah. Hopefully, it has made pups in the meantime to continue the legacy. If not, you'll have to reinvest in a replacement plant.

I limit the agaves-in-residence to a few favorites because I do not want to push my luck with agave encounters, and Einstein has been known to engage in boxing matches with just about anything, including lampshades. I clip off the barbs, but weapon removal has to be ongoing. Agaves are not fast-growing plants, but they gradually make new leaves—and ammunition. On some varieties, the thorns are reminiscent of rhinoceros horns when mature. On others they look like heavy-duty darning needles. Still others have teeth along the entire arm. But there's also beauty in those barbs. Part of the majesty of an agave is the tooth marks each arm leaves embedded after embracing upcoming foliage. You see the shadow of its stranglehold forever imprinted.

Some people find living with sharks to be thrilling. If you are so inclined, agaves will cause no pain in the maintenance department. To treat an agave well (and get the best results), give it a sunny window. In lower light they can stretch rather than forming those remarkable tight buns that make them such an instant crowd pleaser. If the sun is coming from one direction (which is the case with most windows), rotate the plant every two weeks or so. This is not essential, but it will result in a tighter, more comely presentation. That position shifting is really the full extent of your interaction. Agaves can survive on almost no water. Their plump, succulent leaves serve as water-storage units in their arid native habitats. In fact, if agaves have issues such as melting leaves, the problem can usually be traced back to overzealous watering or high humidity. I water mine once a week at most—usually less frequently, depending on the weather.

I don't bother to fertilize my agaves, as they are grown in good potting soil and don't really need the additional food. As a rule, I rarely fertilize my succulents. In their native habitat, life is tough and yet they survive just fine. Why spoil them? Repotting will be a pain—literally. I give mine a deep container and hope they never outgrow it. When they do, I remove all the spines before I make the shift.

I mentioned that it will be curtains for that rosette when agaves bloom. Fortunately, they do not flower often. Agave is also called the century plant because growers originally thought the plant produces blossoms only once every one hundred years. That is not the case. Agaves won't keep you waiting too long and blooming is not a once-in-a-lifetime experience, but most do not flower immediately. When they do blossom, they produce a tall, majestic stalk (aka mast) with flowers at the upper reaches that shoot up several feet in the air. The blossoms themselves are not as eventful as the rest of the package. They would be considered anticlimactic, but when something juts up a few feet in the air from the center of a tiger's jaws, it tends to stop traffic. In this case, that can be a blessing.

AGAVE
Agave

ALSO CALLED **century plant**
EASIEST

SIZE	Ranging from 3 to 36 inches (7 to 91 cm) high, depending on the variety
FOLIAGE	Green, blue-green, or slate; can be variegated
OTHER ATTRIBUTES	Makes rosettes, forms pups, and can produce impressive blossom spikes
EXPOSURE	East, west, or south
WATER REQUIREMENTS	Can tolerate dry soil
OPTIMUM NIGHTTIME TEMPERATURE	50–70°F (10–21°C)
RATE OF GROWTH	Slow
SOIL TYPE	Sandy potting soil, such as cactus and succulent growing mix
FERTILIZING	Unnecessary; if you feel the urge, early spring to late autumn
PROPAGATION	Divide off pups before they develop sharp fangs
ISSUES	Those barbs are truly dangerous; snip them off
COMPANIONS	Display with other succulents of different shapes and sizes for a thrilling freak show

SHARP ARCHITECTURE

Andrea Filippone is the first to acknowledge that agaves have taken over her life. And the fact that she is an architect has everything to do with the preponderance of agaves in her midst. What plant would be more apropos? Andrea is warm and inviting, so her yawning, classical era home comes off as Gothic, although also user-friendly. But it would definitely have the potential to give you goosebumps, with some spaces tightly snug and others massive and flooded with light. It's the sort of place where footsteps echo and botanicals grope. She has furnished it in chairs sans upholstery with their stuffing leaking out. Marble busts of gods and goddesses peer down at you from atop creaking old furniture. You walk on granite slabs rather than floorboards. And you make your way around plants that look mildly menacing. Agaves fit right in.

Andrea can find all sorts of excuses to explain her agave habit: "They're so structural. You don't have to do anything with them, and they make all those pups." Although sleek lines are what got her into agaves, the relationship deepened beyond the quick, admiring glance. Andrea has the soul of a collector. You see the evidence in all the envy-inciting antiques she drags home from trips far and wide, as well as her inventory of plants. Gradually she began her steady climb toward ferreting out just about every agave available in commerce. Her favorite is an immense *Agave americana* hybrid with arms and legs sprawling out several feet in each direction. She swears that it moves daily. "It's so incredibly graceful," she sighs in its presence, "those long arms are so articulate. They twist, they turn. The others don't dance like this one." She may have found her true love, but she's still collecting. After all, there are lots of agaves out there, each has its merits, and they all send out siren songs.

Andrea makes her agaves feel at home. Here she's staged *Agave desmettiana* 'Variegata' beside an unnamed species agave.

AGLAONEMA

n the past, I could never cozy up to aglaonemas. They just never spoke to me. I felt these easily overlooked plants, strongly associated with public spaces, were best left confined to shopping malls. But then my friend and fellow houseplant aficionado James Baggett called to enthuse about them.

I was skeptical at first. Aglaonemas had gone through many decades of blahdom without budging from their simple white-on-green patterned leaves. They are tidy, but that would be the only compliment you could toss in their general direction. However, that was before they got their makeover. James keeps abreast of what's happening, and while I wasn't looking, aglaonemas got pizzazz.

What a novel concept. Take a bulletproof plant, give it a glam wardrobe, and send it out to the garden centers. It's amazing what might happen. People who never tried houseplants before might succeed with something worthwhile. Winter might grow on you.

Homes might be happier. Guests might stop for a second glance. The new aglaonemas are speckled with a confetti of color, striped with bands of deep red and bright pink, and totally jazzed up (indeed, one series is called Jazzed Gems). You would never imagine that they once came from something so yawn-worthy. And countless versions of these new color-jacked Chinese evergreens are being pumped into the market. As if that weren't enough, the leaf-shape inventory has expanded. Some are broader than the prototype, while others have become slender. Your biggest problem will be selecting only one to bring home. The solution? Get several.

Original *Aglaonema commutatum* was by no means a dog. Banded with silver markings and speckling, the leaves of the prototype were everything you might want in a spaceholder. They were tidy, they were predictable, they jumped no hoops, and they were easily overlooked. Not my cup of tea. But some people like roommates with those character traits. If

Aglaonema 'Crete' is one of the new generation of wowzers.

you're looking for more snap, excitement is in the cards.

You don't need to worry that your Chinese evergreen will grow colossal and nudge out its neighbors. Chances are the plant you pick up will remain in a holding pattern for the foreseeable future. That's fine for gardeners who put together a package and want it to look great indefinitely. If you want to maintain the status quo, these are the plants for you. You could pull together a kick line for the windowsill with no fears that it will outgrow your setting tomorrow. An extra leaf here and there is the sum total of an aglaonema's acrobatics.

The original silver aglaonema was totally invincible. If watering slipped your mind, it was fine. Most of the newer hybrids are equally steadfast in their refusal to wilt. But here is a little secret: When an aglaonema is too dry and begging for water, it will stand bolt upright like a head of celery. Once you give it water, its stems fan out to display the inner color of the leaves.

I have been growing

Aglaonema 'Crete', an elegant version with a red streak down the midrib, with complete and unwavering success. It also fits well with my shabby chic decor. I find that red is a common theme with painted antiques, and the crimson streak in 'Crete' echoes the painted furniture throughout my barn, where it happily resides with nearly no maintenance from me. However, 'Sparkling Sarah', with splashes of cream and speckles of pink, has disappointed me (aka died) more than once. Many of the more colorful and speckle-riddled versions are a little more choosy about their light needs. In other words, to get that color, a little more light helps. But don't go too far. No aglaonema craves full sun, which can make the plant scorch. An east- or west-facing window is ideal, especially for bringing out the color in the pink-flushed versions. For the old-fashioned individuals, north is adequate. Sometimes success and a makeover turn an urchin into a prima donna, with the baggage that stardom brings with it.

AGLAONEMA
Aglaonema
ALSO CALLED **Chinese evergreen**
EASY

SIZE	15 inches (38 cm) high
FOLIAGE	Long, thin, and jutting from the base; the original introductions had silver markings, but all sorts of splashed and spangled versions are now available
OTHER ATTRIBUTES	Riveting and tidy presentation on a low-light plant
EXPOSURE	East or west
WATER REQUIREMENTS	Allow soil to dry out slightly between waterings
OPTIMUM NIGHTTIME TEMPERATURE	55–70°F (12–21°C)
RATE OF GROWTH	Slow
SOIL TYPE	Rich, humusy potting soil with compost included
FERTILIZING	Early spring to late autumn
ISSUES	Burns easily in high light; some of the flashier versions are finicky
COMPANIONS	*Selaginella* mosses and *Pilea glauca* can serve as ground covers around the base; grow alongside aspidistras, bromeliads, ferns, and hoyas

Tuck together the new generation of aloe hybrids—here I've bundled 'Vito', 'Silver Edge', 'Silver Ridge', and 'Pink Blush'—and you've got an incomparable easy-care creation.

ALOE

Aloes are basically agaves without weapons. Or, at least, they don't possess heavy artillery, although many do have teeth (*Aloe saponaria* comes to mind). But you can live peacefully beside many aloes without fear of a hurtful attack on a dark and stormy night when you're dashing around to shut the windows and your succulent gets in the way. Many aloes are family safe and free of barbs, unless you back into a flower spike.

Visually, aloes and agaves look fairly similar to the untrained eye. They both fall into the odd-succulents-forming-rosettes department. But to the scientific mind, they aren't even in the same family. Plants are categorized according to their blossom structure, and the differences between aloe flowers and agave blooms put them into different camps.

The most popular, *Aloe vera*, has another perk to recommend it as a roommate: It is useful. Chances are you've encountered it in the pharmacy, as it is a popular medical folk remedy for treating light burns (hence its moniker, burn plant) and other mild skin wounds. I always have an *A. vera* plant in the house.

I consider aloe to be essential, and it's always good when something indispensible is also indestructible. Plus, *Aloe vera* is rather good looking, in a funky sort of way. With thick, succulent leaves growing in rosettes from pups that start as small fans, it could easily serve as a strong architectural element in a room. The plump arms shoot bolt upright and fill vertical space where you need it, like on a side table, beside a stack of books, or next to a floor lamp. Again, aloe is a great substitute for agave where you don't want sharp, pointy objects.

In addition to *Aloe vera*, a slew of other aloes are also readily available. Although to my knowledge *A. vera* is the only version used commercially in pharmaceuticals, the other aloes are even better looking and worth entertaining just for the pleasure of their company. Relatively new on the market is a series of hybrid aloes with small rosettes, intriguing markings, lots of warts, good color, and great names like 'Grassy Lassie', 'Pink Blush', 'Bright Ember', 'Viper', 'Christmas Carol', and 'Starfire'. They are much more compact than *A. vera* and take up a smaller footprint. All are easy to grow, and they make a great combination if you tuck them into a container together. They are one of my favorite fillers for colanders. Not only do they love the many drainage holes, but they also look like an otherworldly moonscape. Or try them in tandem with other succulents of varying textures. They fit anywhere. They can easily go modern, and they are equally apropos in a period home. It's all in the way you package them.

Indoors, aloes need bright light. A windowsill with south-facing sunbeams is ideal. But an east- or west-facing window is a strong second choice. However, if you take your houseplants outdoors in summer, bright light can kill aloes. Although most succulents are fine with full sun, aloes tend to burn, even after the plant appears to be acclimated.

If you're dying to grow an aloe but have only low light, give it a try—you just might succeed with this tolerant plant. But when low light is all you can offer, definitely cut down on watering. In fact, with their fat succulent leaves, aloes are fully able to keep on trucking when you forget to serve drinks.

Aloes like tight containers. Keep the root system crammed (to a point—don't overdo it) or cluster lots of aloes together to prevent the roots from sitting in soggy soil. Along the same line of reasoning, overwatering is a killer. Be sure to let the soil dry out between doses of water. Repotting in a potting soil that has added sand is also helpful for a plant that does not like wet.

The beauty of aloes is they produce babies like rabbits. This trait will make you mighty popular with friends and give you infinite options for hospitality gifts. But don't worry if you lack the time to keep up with the progeny— the pups can remain with the

Aloe saponaria (in the cement container) has barbs, but adorable *A. variegata* 'Gator' is not armed, and it stays midget when confined.

mother plant indefinitely. Of course, the whole caboodle might need repotting sooner. With those fat leaves, the package can also get fairly top heavy (without even trying hard, Einstein has managed to send my aloe into a tailspin more than once). A container with ballast down below is the way to go.

Most people would be perfectly pleased with those chubby leaves. But if you give aloes bright light, they add some wacky flower spikes to the hoopla. This tends to occur in midwinter, right when you desperately need something really bizarre and botanical to take place. The spike pokes up from the center of the plant like a porpoise nose breaking the waves, then erupts into a spire of colorful tubular blossoms that will have you calling up your friends to beg them to come over. Boasting rights are part of what houseplants promise. Go ahead. Feel the pride.

ALOE
Aloe

ALSO CALLED **burn plant**
EASIEST

SIZE	Ranging from 4 to 36 inches (10 to 91 cm) high, depending on the variety
FOLIAGE	Succulent with typically pale green leaves; hybrids have warts and colorful markings
OTHER ATTRIBUTES	Makes rosettes, forms pups, and can produce blossoms
EXPOSURE	South, east, or west
WATER REQUIREMENTS	Can tolerate dry soil
OPTIMUM NIGHTTIME TEMPERATURE	50–70°F (10–21°C)
RATE OF GROWTH	Slow
SOIL TYPE	Sandy potting soil, such as cactus and succulent growing mix
FERTILIZING	Unnecessary; if you feel the urge, feed in early spring to late autumn
PROPAGATION	Divide off pups
ISSUES	Can sunburn when put outdoors in bright sun
COMPANIONS	Display with fellow aloes or other succulents; combination planters are an option

ALTERNANTHERA

I gave *Alternanthera ficoidea* 'Chinese Afro' up for dead, but it revived. That's fortitude for you.

thought my *Alternanthera ficoidea* 'Chinese Afro' was a goner, I really did. After I committed the cardinal sin of bringing it out from the house into direct sun one summer day, it swooned. And it was the type of fainting act that appeared to be terminal. The only thing that kept me from tossing the ugly mess was sheer laziness. Fortunately, procrastination is a trait that often plays to my advantage.

Actually, I was in mourning, because I really liked that plant. It had formed a little mass of squiggly shiny green leaves that cre ated a tidy bun. I'm not sure what "Chinese" relates to, as the parent plant is native to South America, but the "Afro" correlation is a clear reference to the hairdo. *Alternanthera ficoidea* 'Chinese Afro' is a tiny plant. You could easily use it to make a miniature container garden. To give it some bulk and a sense of presence, I put it in a hefty long tom. I chose a container with a smallish mouth circumference so I would not be tempted to overwater the plant. Plus, a long tom

does not increase its footprint on the windowsill but makes a substantial physical statement. I use this ploy frequently.

'Chinese Afro' surprised me by failing to succumb. After a couple of weeks I began to notice new growth. That was all the encouragement I needed to rush into nurse mode. I pulled it into the shade, cleaned off the browned foliage, and kept it watered. A month later you would never know it was once a burn victim. Since then, the plant has proved itself to be fairly easy on every front. I put some other alternantheras to the test, and in most instances they passed with flying colors.

Jazzy hues are one of the perks that alternantheras offer, especially the flashier versions, often known as Joseph's coat and its brethren. Although 'Chinese Afro' is plain green—albeit a shiny and very appealing green—other *Alternanthera ficoidea* hybrids add to the spectrum. 'Chartreuse' is bright lime, 'Red Threads' is a mass of pencil-thin deep maroon leaves, and 'Party Time' has

ALTERNANTHERA

Alternanthera

ALSO CALLED Joseph's coat
EASY

SIZE	Ranging from 5 to 12 inches (12 to 30 cm) high
FOLIAGE	'Chinese Afro' has shiny green twisted leaves; others have chartreuse, burgundy, and pink foliage
OTHER ATTRIBUTES	Can be used to fill around the base of taller plants
EXPOSURE	South is optimal, but east or west also works
WATER REQUIREMENTS	Keep soil moderately moist; keep water off foliage
OPTIMUM NIGHTTIME TEMPERATURE	50–65°F (10–18°C)
RATE OF GROWTH	Medium
SOIL TYPE	Rich, humusy potting soil with compost included
FERTILIZING	Early spring to late autumn
PROPAGATION	Easily rooted by cuttings, like coleus
ISSUES	Tightly massed foliage can lead to rot
COMPANIONS	Agaves, aloes, geraniums, kalanchoes, rhipsalis, and senecios

bicolored leaves that are sharply divided between green and hot pink. All are surprisingly suitable for life as houseplants. Even more amazingly, all are fairly easy if you give them bright light and don't overwater. The exception is 'White Carpet'. It has a dense mass of little variegated leaves all squished together, and their close proximity tends to invite problems.

For alternantheras, the foliage is the thing. None of the versions currently available has flowers worth noting. But if you like blossoms that look like tiny white clover nuggets, they can be part of the package. Think of gomphrena (also in the amaranth family) without the great flower colors.

Aside from 'Chinese Afro', alternantheras are not generally marketed as houseplants, but don't let that dissuade you from trying them. In the garden, they are often used as bedding plants or for accenting the edge of a border. Take your cue from the garden and try tucking them around the base of a plant with a naked stem, like a ficus. However, be sure they receive fairly good light, because they need it to form a tight wad of leaves. If you have a south-facing window, all the better, but east or west will also work. Pruning keeps the presentation sharp, although most alternantheras remain fairly compact without a lot of help.

If you need an infusion of color in your indestructible configuration, alternantheras are for you. Some could almost be called flamboyant. If you give them a smart presentation, they will turn heads. Part of the beauty of this plant is that you can pick some up for a song as summer annuals, and then just whisk them inside when the season begins to fade. As for 'Chinese Afro', it is indestructible with a twist.

Alternanthera dentata 'Red Threads' doesn't look like a trouper, but it's amazingly stoic indoors.

ARALIA

Try combining false aralia (*Schefflera elegantissima* 'Gold Crest') beside *Polyscias* cultivars, and underplant it with *Pilea depressa* to create a mini forest.

Sometimes, at the end of a long day, I just want to go into the woods. You know the feeling, I'm sure. Maybe you've been pounding the pavement all afternoon, or perhaps you've been pounding the keyboard, but you feel the need to be enveloped in the cool, dark succor of nature. Unfortunately, it isn't always possible. For example, right now I would need to shovel 3 feet of concrete-heavy snow to get anywhere. Plodding down to the goat barn requires fifteen minutes of gearing up with a couple of wool scarves, extra socks, and double-insulated mittens. Once outside, I can just about unthaw the water before the chilblains set in. I won't be doing any actual forest hiking for a while. But I can take the virtual route.

Stationed where I can monitor its progress on a regular basis, in my most trafficked route between the office and the kitchen, is a little false aralia forest-in-a-window-box. It takes up less than a foot of space, but I don't know where I would be without it. It's my meditation unit. I look at the mini trees growing in a tiny grove matted by green pilea tumbling over somebody-shrank-the-boulders, and all is well with the world.

The false aralia forest is my vicarious walk in the woods, and I make that journey whenever I can find an excuse to spend a few minutes putting myself into the scene. I love going there in my mind, but I don't necessarily like to spend time fussing over the package. The little false aralias, *Schefflera elegantissima*, qualify for the job on the strength of their smaller-than-life tree stature. They start off as little cuttings resembling a tree, and the similarity gets more pronounced with time. But they are also delightfully low maintenance. They provide a nature walk without any upkeep.

You're probably wondering why I didn't cover false aralia in the schefflera section. Truth is, they keep reclassifying the plant. Until today, I knew false aralia as *Dizygotheca elegantissima*. Maybe the powers that be felt sorry for our mouths, because they

False aralia, *Schefflera elegantissima*, is a quaint stand-in for a mini tree.

changed that name. Apparently they added to the identity crisis by addressing it as *Plerandra elegantissima* along the way. No matter what it's called, the juvenile version of this plant looks like a tiny tree with skeleton-thin leaves along a little trunk. The bronze leaves come in segments of five or three fingers. For the cultivar 'Gold Crest', cream bands run along their edges with a red midrib. They're very fetching, and very easy.

There are other, equally adaptable aralias, but the names are a terrible muddle. You'll be more apt to hunt them up under the common names. Ming aralia, *Polyscias fruticosa* (for now), also looks like a mini tree with clusters of curled leaves around a woody stem. It's more prone to drop leaves under stress, but it is a fairly easy, low-light indoor plant that will slowly become a larger specimen. Other intriguing spins on the aralia theme have white-edged, rounded leaves. Blink and another few will be introduced.

Most of the aralias I have worked with tend to be slow growing. You won't be racing against time to keep the plant in check when you enlist it for your forest-in-a-pot. Over the long haul they become little bushes and require a sizable footprint, but that will take years. Meanwhile, they all prefer low light; an east- or west-facing window is ideal. They don't need high humidity, they wilt only when you parch them severely, and they aren't prone to insect problems. Your virtual nature experience can be a definite exhale without any stress. Wouldn't that be a walk in the park?

ARALIA
Schefflera and *Polyscias*
ALSO CALLED false aralia, Ming aralia
EASIEST

SIZE	Remains 5 to 12 inches (12 to 30 cm) high for a year or more before becoming a small bush
FOLIAGE	Leaves come in sets of so-called fingers from the stem; several varieties are variegated
OTHER ATTRIBUTES	Can be used to mimic a mini tree in a combination planter
EXPOSURE	East or west
WATER REQUIREMENTS	Keep soil moderately moist
OPTIMUM NIGHTTIME TEMPERATURE	50–65°F (10–18°C)
RATE OF GROWTH	Slow
SOIL TYPE	Rich, humusy potting soil with compost included
FERTILIZING	Early spring to late autumn
PROPAGATION	By cuttings, but woody rooting hormone might be helpful
ISSUES	Can get scale
COMPANIONS	Bromeliads, ivies, mosses, nerve plants, peperomias, and pileas

ASPIDISTRA

A star-studded spin on the plain green version, *Aspidistra elatior* 'Milky Way' is all the rage.

Some plants in this book have received a bad rap. Some of you snicker when you see a sansevieria in a dark corner, and you don't treat dracaenas with all due respect. Well, watch out. One day you might need to retract any snide remarks sent in that philodendron's direction. A much-maligned ivy might stage a comeback and return to bask in the sunbeams of brilliant coolness, just like the aspidistra. Then you'll get your comeuppance.

Aspidistras were once omnipresent. In the early twentieth century they were a hackneyed symbol for all that was banal in the status quo. H. E. Bates's novella *An Aspidistra in Babylon* chronicles an unsuspecting young woman's life before a not-entirely-trustworthy soldier shakes up an existence that was "dull as one of the aspidistras that cluttered our...little boarding house." During the First and Second World Wars, aspidistras stood for everything that was dusty. Every room had an aspidistra, and nobody paid them an ounce of attention.

Nowadays aspidistras have a certain cachet.

Well, maybe the old dark green version, *Aspidistra elatior*, hasn't made the scene yet. It's still a bore. But 'Milky Way' has definitely gained the secret handshake into the halls of coolness. The only difference is a constellation of irregular flecks mottling the long buff leaves that jut straight from the soil. It is slightly shorter than the prototype, and its leaves stand about 15 inches (38 cm) high. The variegated versions, with slashes of white running the length of the leaves, are virtual collector's items, especially if they have major markings as opposed to tiny rivulets of white. If you really want to impress guests, try seeking out *Aspidistra elatior* 'Asahi'. This Japanese introduction (the name translates as "morning sun") has an inverted pure white chevron mark blazing through the tip of each spathe-like leaf. It is totally beguiling when you have a mature plant with a bristle of leaves that look like they were dipped in a bucket of white paint.

There is absolutely no

abracadabra involved in growing an aspidistra. Depending on whom you ask, aspidistras are called barbershop plants or cast iron plants. Both nicknames give you a hint at the fortitude for which they are famed. It's hard to undermine an aspidistra. It tolerates almost closet-like conditions in the light department, although very bright sun can cause slight burning. Forget to water for a week? No problem. Forget to water for two weeks? Still no reaction. If you keep up the total neglect, the leaf tips will begin to turn crispy brown in protest. They will probably succumb eventually if subjected to severe torment, but maybe not. (I cannot say for sure because they tend to be too expensive for torture testing.)

Display your aspidistra with pride. There is no reason to stuff it into an overlooked place in the floor plan. Mine lives beside my comfy chair, where the long speckled leaves of 'Milky Way' brush against me when I turn on the reading light. The speckles also pick up the creamy white in the plain-vanilla upholstery. I gave it a painted pot to add another level of interest. And when Einstein takes a swat, there are no repercussions. The tough foliage just sways.

The trick to an aspidistra (if there is one) lies in getting it to a sufficiently impressive size. This can take years. An aspidistra with just a few leaves is not going to garner any kind of compliments, no matter how variegated its leaves or how smart its presentation. My advice is to invest in a sizable plant, then give it the grand display it deserves. And, for Pete's sake, dust it once in a while.

ASPIDISTRA
Aspidistra

ALSO CALLED barbershop plant, cast iron plant
EASIEST

SIZE	Ranging from 15 to 24 inches (38 to 61 cm) high
FOLIAGE	Tall, straight, and lance-like dark green leaves with various markings
OTHER ATTRIBUTES	Famously indomitable
EXPOSURE	East, west, or north
WATER REQUIREMENTS	Keep soil lightly moist but not soggy
OPTIMUM NIGHTTIME TEMPERATURE	50–80°F (10–27°C)
RATE OF GROWTH	Very slow
SOIL TYPE	Any old potting soil will do; ideally good potting soil with compost included
FERTILIZING	Early spring to late autumn, but that's gravy
ISSUES	Sometimes hard to find and very slow growing; leaf tips can brown from lack of water
COMPANIONS	Ferns and mosses make a wonderful textural counterpoint in a display

BEGONIA

Begonia 'Black Truffles' has an incredibly long blooming spree. It continues flowering from midwinter until summer.

Begonias, indestructible? Easy for me to say: Begonia is almost my middle name. Over my long and deep green past, I have grown just about every begonia known to humanity. Well, not really, because there are upward of 900 species out there, not to mention the thousands of cultivars created by folks like me, who feel 900 is not nearly enough. But during my twenty-five-year tenure at Logee's Greenhouses in Danielson, Connecticut, I curated the begonia collection happily and intensively. The assemblage originally included the rhizomatous, rex, cane, angel wing, semperflorens, semi-tuberous, tuberous, and hiemalis groups. I do not recommend them all as bulletproof, but some are pretty tough cookies.

All begonias are irresistible. But you need to know which members of this alluring family are toughest so you can succeed without shedding tears. First, you need to focus on the rhizomatous group. This is where you will find the wonderful hand-me-down begonias you inherited from your grandmother. Before central heat, indoor plumbing, and all the other modern conveniences, a few stalwart begonias were chugging along in less-than-ideal home settings. The two stars of the show were pond lily begonia, *Begonia* 'Erythrophylla' (aka beefsteak begonia), and star begonia, *B.* 'Ricinifolia' (aka castor bean begonia, probably the first begonia hybrid). You likely know these two most-wanted heirlooms on sight. Pond lily begonia has smooth, shiny, round leaves with a bronze cast. Star begonia has (you guessed it) star-shaped green leaves with a chenille of bristly red hairs on the leaf petioles. Both are nearly unkillable, although they can come down with powdery mildew if continually subjected to poor air circulation and dank conditions. But generally they are impervious. And although powdery mildew defaces some leaves, the plant will survive the affliction. In general, the only problems gardeners face with these vintage rhizomatous begonias is how to give old, gnarly plants new life.

While we're on the subject, here's how to rejuvenate rhizomatous begonias and give them further zest. First, cut back the old rhizomes. Rhizomatous begonias send up growth from arms and legs that creep along the top of the soil. These swollen appendages are not particularly handsome; indeed, they look slightly arthritic. But they are your targets for makeover surgery. Do not cut them back to their fat, woody origins. Instead, try to save some younger sections and remove straggly growth. If you do it correctly, you will have a newly invigorated plant. It's like molting. And, of course, if you don't mind the straggly presentation, there's no harm in leaving your inherited begonia alone.

Pond lily and castor bean begonias are just the beginning. The plant has come a long way. There are loads of rhizomatous begonias out there, and many are equally rock solid. In a family that can be dicey, many are not prima donnas. *Begonia*

Not only are leaf shapes wildly varied in the rhizomatous begonia group, but the size range also runs the gamut. *Begonia* 'Cowardly Lion' (far left) is medium size compared to miniature *B*. 'Bethlehem Star' (front) and *B*. 'Palomar Prince'.

'Zip', *B*. 'River Nile', *B*. 'Tiger Kitten', and many others aim to please. These add some dash to your home with their colorful, mottled, or striped leaves. There are some truly challenging rare species of rhizomatous begonias, but most of the readily available rhizomatous are a cakewalk.

Flowers are also in your cards with the rhizomatous clan, especially in late winter, when they send up wands of tiny colorful blooms to quell the pangs of cabin fever. The pink, salmon, or white blossoms are adorable, and they make all the difference at a time of year when you're starving for color.

Although rhizomatous begonias are relatively easy, they will not endure constantly wet foliage or consistently damp roots. Do not drench this plant. In fact, if you lean in the drier direction, your relationship will be better. Another trick is to aim the watering can at the soil surface rather than the leaves. Begonias don't like wet foliage. Do not grant them overly generous root room, as there is not a begonia on Earth that likes to swim in its pot. Their root systems grow horizontally, so most prefer shallow containers to deep pots.

The majority of begonias like to be stationed in an east- or west-facing window where they receive good light but not baking sun. A north-facing window is pushing it. South works in winter, but can scorch in summer. Begonias do not like chilly conditions.

When working begonias into the indoor scenery, I play up their texture because many have furry, eyelashed leaves. Since I'm a collector, the dialogue is often between several begonias grown side by side. But ferns and orchids are good growing mates too. The tapestry that results can read well with upholstered furniture and nubby throws for the sofa. Begonias work equally well in a Victorian home or a contemporary scene. Put a begonia in a spare modern setting and its leaf shape says a lot, even in a limited space.

Coming in at second place behind rhizomatous begonias would be the angel wing branch of the cane group. You have probably encountered these majestic plants in your travels. Their leaves come in all sizes, they tend to be wing shaped, and they can have intriguing markings. Flower umbels can be immense and colorful, and they hold steady in pristine condition for weeks. Although angel wings are not that difficult to grow, they require some strategic and frequent pruning to keep the plant appealing. Otherwise you will be staring at a forest of naked stems with leaves at their tips. It's not a happy picture. With pruning, they can be quite elegant. This is the plant for anyone who is fond of taking cuttings.

Whichever way you go with begonias, good things are in store. They offer diversity beyond your wildest dreams. You could explore this family for decades and not grow even slightly bored. I know this from experience.

BEGONIA
Begonia
EASY

SIZE	Ranging from 3 to 30 inches (7 to 76 cm) high
FOLIAGE	Extremely diverse, with all sorts of leaf shapes, textures, and sizes available
OTHER ATTRIBUTES	Midwinter blossoms
EXPOSURE	East or west
WATER REQUIREMENTS	Allow soil to dry out between waterings
OPTIMUM NIGHTTIME TEMPERATURE	55–70°F (12–21°C)
RATE OF GROWTH	Medium
SOIL TYPE	Rich, humusy, peaty potting soil with compost included
FERTILIZING	Early spring to late autumn
ISSUES	Powdery mildew can be a problem
COMPANIONS	African violets, bromeliads, ferns, mosses, nerve plants, plectranthus, and any other low-light individuals

MORE, MORE, MORE: PROPAGATING BEGONIAS

If you want to share your begonias with admirers, it's easier than you think. Begonias are particularly simple to propagate, and there are several ways to do it.

With rhizomatous begonias, you have the option of clipping off one of the creeping arms and legs that wander on the surface of the container. They usually already have roots attached that anchor them to the soil. Simply pull off that leg (if it has growth on the tip, all the better) and lay it on top of a new container with half the rhizome and the roots buried. Young rhizomes will make handsome new plants faster than old, woody individuals. But any version should work.

You can also use rhizomatous and rex begonia leaves to make new plants. One method is to take off the leaf with its leaf stem, dip it in rooting hormone, and stick it in new soil like an umbrella, firming the soil around the base of the stem and watering the soil around it. This method takes longer; it is usually one to two months before

little plantlets appear clustered around the leaf stem. During that time, keep it in a cloche to raise humidity.

Leaf wedges are also an option with rhizomatous and rex begonia leaves. Cut off a leaf, remove its leaf stem, and divide it into pie-like wedges, making sure the middle sinus is included in each wedge. Dip the pointed tip in rooting hormone, push one third of the wedge into soil, firm it in, and water it. As with other leaf cuttings, a cloche helps to keep humidity high during rooting.

You can easily root angel wing and cane type begonias by cuttings. Cut the stem a few inches from the tip and strip off or diminish side leaves to prevent wilting. Dip the stem in rooting hormone, firm the stem into soil, and put it in a cloche for a few weeks while roots are formed. This is a great gift to share with friends who admire your menagerie. And what a resourceful way to recycle cuttings when your cat has caused an "accident."

BROMELIADS

My nephew is murder on houseplants. He means well, I'm sure. I have a photo of Ben as a wee tyke eagerly aiming a watering can at a houseplant. But I feel certain that was the last time he ever watered a plant. He is now in his twenties.

Lack of watering skills aside, Ben has the urge. His first impulse upon coming through my door is to scoop up Einstein in a vigorous hug, then head over to the houseplant menagerie to make appreciative noises and pluck Calamondin oranges. Later that evening, he regales me with gory tales of the fates of all the poor photosynthesizing souls that I sent home with him on previous visits. Ben is the acid test for indestructible. From now on, he gets air plants and only air plants.

It takes talent to kill an air plant. If the Purple Heart medal was handed out to heroic houseplants, tillandsias would win it hands down. They would work for Ben because they need water only once a week. Air plants can also survive without containers. They literally lie out in the air sans soil. The easiest way to grow a tillandsia is in a bowl. I like glass because it twinkles and it gives me a clear window on the whole plant from anywhere in the room. Many people grow air plants in dangling hand blown glass orbs that look absolutely fantastic hanging around. I also find cake stands with slight indents to serve as water reservoirs for weekly dunking, or I pick up antique compotes with elegant etched markings in the glass. And who can stop at just one? I group them together for a massive sparkle, and the plants are already in the perfect receptacle to be filled with water once a week. I submerge them for a few hours and then toss off the water, and they're good to go for another week or so. What I don't tell Ben (because he'll push it) is that they could probably go a little longer.

And that's it for tillandsias. No further fuss whatsoever. They are absolutely bizarre, Disney-caliber plants. They look like sea urchins,

You can find bromeliads that take up a big chunk of space, but *Vriesea fenestralis*, cryptanthus, and *Quesnelia marmorata* remain small, while air plant *Tillandsia xerographica* (the curly silver number) doesn't even need a container.

hedgehogs, or other oddball phenomena that might play feature roles in sci-fi flicks. There are several varieties out there, the most common of which is *Tillandsia ionanthe*. *Tillandsia caput-medusae* (which looks like a Medusa head of squiggly snakes) is a close second on the popularity meter. And *T. xerographica*, with its flat silver leaves forming a rosette and swooping down into a curlicue, is a work of art and easy to find as well as grow. If you don't live anywhere near a good garden center, take heart. Tillandsias ship seamlessly for all the reasons that

render them nephew-proof.

Although tillandsias are the toughest members of the bromeliad family, the whole clan is fairly streetwise. Other members should be anchored in soil and containers, but most will tolerate long spates of negligence. As a rule they don't like soggy soil, so if you're prone to overwatering, stand off. Along those lines, they prefer a well-drained potting medium rather than a mucky one. Some folks grow them in shredded moss, but I find that an overall good potting soil works. The trick lies in keeping the root system fairly

tightly potted rather than being overly generous with root room. Bromeliads make minimal roots, so they tend to swim in large containers.

The beauty of bromeliads is their diversity. Like tillandsias, they are arrestingly majestic in an art-installment sort of way. Off the top of my head I could rattle off a slew of favorites, including *Vriesea hieroglyphica*, *Quesnelia marmorata* (aka Grecian urn plant because of the graceful curves of its long, flat leaves), any *Neoregelia*, and *Billbergia nutans* (aka queen's tears or friendship plant, with navy blue stripes on its flowerscape). The leaf coloration and markings on these plants embrace the full spectrum of wonderful. They have speckling, spots, marbleizing, shading, bars, and bands. And they're addictive. You really cannot collect just one; I struggle to limit myself to a mere half dozen. Most of these have rosettes of leaves that form a vase at the top, and the vase loves to be filled with water. In fact, it's an easy way to keep the plants quenched and happy (Ben, take heed). If you fill the vase with water, you are giving your bromeliad its drink. But please remember the splash effect when you're moving them around. I have taken many inadvertent baths while shuffling my bromeliads, and the water sitting in those tubes is definitely unpleasant.

For my favorites, I have remained within the more user-friendly realms of the bromeliad clan. However, there is a contingent with seriously sharp artillery. Dyckias, with their razor-sharp teeth, are downright dangerous. Ditto for orthophytums and ananas (aka pineapple). My friends at Landcraft Environments on Long Island gave me a cunning little *Ananas nanus*. It produces tiny little pineapples snuggled close to slender, shark-like leaves. It's a heartthrob, for sure, but you don't want to stage it anywhere in proximity to a window that needs to be opened and shut on a regular basis. Instead, I bring these plants into the body of the room and play them off one another, or I combine them with ferns to soften their sleek surfaces and lines. Some aechmeas can get pretty large and handsome with broad gray-silver leaves, and they can become a strong stand-alone architectural element. If you give the plant an urn to match, your home could look like Versailles.

Although there are plenty of bromeliads with bristles, I've never met one that had a prickly personality. They are all relatively eager to please. Do not overwater them, and your relationship will be groovy. Better to water once a week or so. Nephews, take notice—weekly does not mean never.

BROMELIADS
Ananas, Billbergia, Cryptanthus, Neoregelia, Quesnelia, Tillandsia, and *Vriesea*

ALSO CALLED **air plants, urn plants, friendship plants**
EASIEST

SIZE	Ranging from 3 to 36 inches (7 to 91 cm) high
FOLIAGE	Varying greatly in configuration, but frequently long and forming a vase; often grayish but sometimes green with all sorts of gorgeous markings
OTHER ATTRIBUTES	Air plants need no soil to grow
EXPOSURE	East or west
WATER REQUIREMENTS	Weekly works for most; with vase-forming varieties, fill the vase with water
OPTIMUM NIGHTTIME TEMPERATURE	55–70°F (12–21°C)
RATE OF GROWTH	Very slow
SOIL TYPE	Humusy, peaty potting soil with compost included
FERTILIZING	Early spring to late autumn
ISSUES	None
COMPANIONS	Begonias, dracaenas, ferns, ivies, mosses, and slipper orchids

Come winter, you might find yourself yearning for some grass. *Carex morrowii* 'Ice Ballet' gives you the blades you need without the fuss.

CAREX

Einstein is feeling destructive this morning. So far he has taken a bite out of a broom handle and a trowel—or, at least, he tried to gnaw them down to size. I sent him over to the carex and let him vent there. Indestructible has another definition around here. Anything on the premises has to withstand the Einstein test.

I should qualify that statement, because some of the plants in this book are poisonous to cats. Einstein is not a plant nibbler. He's a swatter and a batter and a shredder and a bouncer, but he's not an ingester. However, I keep poisonous plants at a respectful distance from his flying leap. No point in taking risks. Fortunately, none of the grasses I grow are in the poisonous category. Indeed, Einstein has his own little cat grass farm just for grazing. Other grasses get slashed and crushed at regular intervals (why sleep on a mound of pillows when you can flatten the resident carex?).

The carex is the scapegoat in the family, and it looks lovingly pawed, rearranged, and whipped up as a result. But it survives. Although the various grasses indoors don't have the buzz-cut look that would make them appear totally cool, peace and harmony reign as long as Einstein is happy.

In my home, I grow ornamental grasses beyond the sedge group. But I would categorize most as just a tad more challenging than your average carex because of their (nearly) insatiable thirst for water. For example, there's fountain grass, *Pennisetum setaceum* 'Rubrum', which I grow indoors. Other people measure their worth by the leather chairs and trendy pillows in their midst. If I make a late-night run into the kitchen and feel the soft brush of a pennisetum plume against my face, I figure life is good. Einstein is with me on this. He gets his vicarious fresh-air experience by being tickled by grass catkins and batting back at the pennisetum. The plant has also been a thrifty investment in time. It might require innumerable trips to the sink with the watering can, but just think of all the hours I might otherwise have to spend dangling cat toys. The pennisetum is a free catsitter and Einstein-entertainment station. Also in that category is fiber-optic grass, *Isolepis cernua*, which forms a dancing tuft just begging for a few fisticuffs.

Fescue is another favorite on the home front for my pawed sidekick and me. Einstein finds it infinitely smushable, especially blue-bladed *Festuca glauca* in all its very, very subtle nuances (can anybody tell the difference between the cultivars on the market?). Even half-flattened by a cat who thinks he's still kitten-size, I find it looks a whole lot better indoors in a container than outside. Inside it goes about its steady business of doing absolutely nothing with the same lackadaisical attitude as in the front yard. It is no trouble whatsoever, if you discount fluffing occasionally and removing thatches of browned leaves. In other words, it never looks ravishing, but who needs beautiful when you've got 10 pounds of fur balanced on top of you?

The carex clan is wonderfully forgiving about water. They are not camels in the same sense

QUENCHING THIRST

I am not prone to overwatering my houseplants. If anything, I tend to water too sparingly. But I know some of you just love to furnish drinks. In that case, certain plants in this book are for you. Get yourself a carex, fern, iresine, or moss, and you'll be blissful. On the other hand, for those of you who need a few pointers on how to keep thirsty plants quenched, here goes.

When you're potting the plant, leave plenty of room between the soil level and the rim of the container so you can fill it sufficiently. In the case of carex and other ornamental grasses, you might consider leaving more fill-up space than you would normally afford. Also, be sure to keep the plant repotted. Cramped roots will beg for water so frequently that they can be a nuisance. A quick repotting will save you loads of time.

Give thirsty plants a sufficiently deep saucer so they can slurp up water from below when necessary. In fact, if a thirsty plant dries out, soak it from below so the soil will work its sponge action rather than send the water down the sides and straight out the drainage hole. To prevent this, visit frequently with your watering can.

I keep a full watering can near thirsty plants. When I'm walking by and notice that a plant is dry but its neighbors are not, I can shoot a stream of water in the right direction. It also helps if you have a mom who telephones frequently. Perfect opportunity to water plants while chatting.

as the ponytail palm, but you will not be doing relays with the watering can at their behest. Sometimes I push the limit, and I have learned they can be provoked to turn brown. But the beauty of carexes is that they forgive and forget. You can cut them back and they look even better than before. The fact that grasses just love a haircut is nothing new to the lawnmower clan. But it does translate nicely indoors.

Carex come in all shapes and size profiles. You could get *Carex flagellifera* 'Toffee Twist' and it would form a shower of tawny blades from the central base, like a pageboy hairdo. It looks wonderful in a squat urn (I put mine in a zinc container on the floor and let Einstein climb up into a soft grass-blade bed—it beats investing in a plush faux shearling throw). Or you could do *C. caryophyllea* 'Beatlemania' with the reassurance that it would remain pretty much a tidy mini mop-top if contained in a tight pot with restricted root room. Whatever carex you select, they all instill the sense of garden in our homes

and offices. Wrack my brain though I might, I cannot think of a carex that is not apropos for inside. Even *C. morrowii* 'Ice Ballet' works.

When hosting the larger members of the genus ('Ice Ballet' being a good example), I suggest giving them generous root room in their container. I am growing one in a vessel that I have not drilled with drainage holes, and it's doing just fine. The ample roots slurp up any extra moisture and keep the soil from going anaerobic, which leads to that sickening swampy smell in undrained pots. Of course, size might be a factor in your selection of an appropriate carex to bring home. The 24-inch-tall (61 cm) *Carex muskingumensis* might be more grass than you care to host.

For exciting spins, I try to hunt up variegated or colorful grasses to keep me riveted. But make your own choices. As for Einstein, he really does not care what color his grasses come in. Anything that furthers the daily swipe is okay with him.

CAREX
Carex

ALSO CALLED **sedge**
EASIEST

SIZE	Ranging from 5 to 12 inches (12 to 30 cm) high
FOLIAGE	Spiky or gracefully arched; often variegated
OTHER ATTRIBUTES	Satisfies your cat's aggressive tendencies without getting shredded
EXPOSURE	East, west, or south
WATER REQUIREMENTS	Very thirsty
OPTIMUM NIGHTTIME TEMPERATURE	50–60°F (10–15°C)
RATE OF GROWTH	Slow
SOIL TYPE	Rich, humusy potting soil capable of retaining moisture with compost included
FERTILIZING	Early spring to late autumn
ISSUES	Requires a lot of water, plus removal of browning blades
COMPANIONS	Not a great plant for combo containers because of its drinking habit, but grow alongside geraniums, hoyas, peperomias, and rhipsalis

CHRISTMAS CACTUS

The color range in Christmas cactus has expanded immensely over the years. *Schlumbergera* 'Orange Flame' is one of the brightest.

Deep in everyone's past lies a Christmas cactus. Close your eyes and go back in your memory to a winter of your youth. Somewhere in that picture a Christmas cactus is lurking. Maybe it was not the center of attention. Perhaps the gift-wrapped boxes are the focus. But when the plant began to open its blossoms, you finally noticed it.

My friend Mary Danielson's Christmas cactus was magnificent. Mary's dining room was a modest farmhouse affair, with stacks of *Farmers' Almanac* stuffed into corners and an amaryllis ceremoniously positioned in the center of the table. The Christmas cactus sat by the window, a massive hulk with a full burden of buds waiting to pop. More than the eggnog, more than the sprinkle-studded sugar cookies, I remember that plant.

The Christmas cactus fills a niche. Early winter can get a little sparse in the blossom department. The season is not totally devoid of flowers, but it needs all the help it can get. Amaryllis waits in the wings, but not necessarily for Christmas. And flaming Katy (*Kalanchoe blossfeldiana*) is obligingly performing. But Christmas cactus is a marquee-quality soloist.

Although it looks like a succulent, Christmas cactus is technically in the Cactaceae. When I first got into the business, there was a lot of confusion between Thanksgiving cactus and Christmas cactus, and neither ever bloomed on schedule. They've been bred together now, so the performance run has been extended and the color range is phenomenal. You get hues in *Schlumbergera buckleyi* like you've never even seen in the rainbow. Sunset oranges, Spanish shawl reds, flaming yellows, pearly whites with ballet pink flares. You will want the full spectrum, and you can have it. Christmas cacti bloom very young. You can pluck a cutting and stuff it into an itty-bitty pot and it will burst into bud—if the timing is right. It also makes a great gift, especially if you give it a glam presentation.

The flowers deserve a trumpet fanfare. As mentioned, the color range is incredible, and blooms are shaped like dragons with flaring gills and gaping mouths. They are outrageous. They are also huge. We're talking 2 to 3 inches (5 to 7 cm) long. And, on a mature plant, there are plenty.

A Christmas cactus can last forever. Get a little cutting, and it might outlive you. They become larger and larger. They also get heavier and heavier and more unwieldy to maneuver as they add bulk to the blossom display every year. A Christmas cactus comes on strong from the smallest cutting and continues to throw out fireworks. What more could you ask?

I nearly forgot to mention that Christmas cactus requires almost no maintenance. Feel free to get one right before the busy holidays; it won't take a chunk out of your time. In fact, if the Christmas cactus outlives you, it won't be burden to your heirs. The more you fuss, the less happy it becomes. Better to just keep it in its original container; let the segmented, flat, ribbon-like stems fill out; and forget it. Water it when the soil is dry—don't let those little segmented stems shrivel. But the Christmas cactus tolerates a lot of forgetfulness before showing any signs of discomfort. And it does not need a bright south-facing window. In fact, it can burn in too much light in summer. An east- or west-facing window will suffice.

Christmas cactus doesn't bloom throughout the year. It blossoms during winter, when you most need flowers. Whether it opens for Thanksgiving or Christmas can be a little unpredictable and the subject of much confusion ("Is it a Thanksgiving cactus or a Christmas cactus?"). But it does perform when light levels are low, which is more than you can say for most of us.

CHRISTMAS CACTUS
Schlumbergera buckleyi
EASIEST

SIZE	Ranging from 12 to 15 inches (30 to 38 cm) high
FOLIAGE	Flat, segmented leaves
OTHER ATTRIBUTES	Incredibly large flowers, in profusion, that look like dragonheads
EXPOSURE	South, east, or west
WATER REQUIREMENTS	Can tolerate dry soil, but don't overdo it
OPTIMUM NIGHTTIME TEMPERATURE	50–70°F (10–21°C)
RATE OF GROWTH	Medium
SOIL TYPE	Sandy potting soil, such as cactus and succulent growing mix
FERTILIZING	Unnecessary; if you feel the urge, early spring to late autumn
ISSUES	Unpredictable bloom times if you absolutely need it for the holidays in future years
COMPANIONS	Too large to share a container, but display it with fellow succulents, rhipsalis, and senecios

CROTON

If you didn't recognize *Codiaeum variegatum* 'Revolutions' as a croton, don't be embarrassed. It's a totally different animal with a twist, as well as a great companion for slipper orchids.

Initially, croton did not make the cut for this book. *Codiaeum variegatum* var. *pictum*, the flagship of the family, failed to qualify because it is not particularly easy to grow indoors. Sure, you would love to invite something dressed in such snappy attire into your home. Who would not want that unabashed party animal nearby, with its big, thick, leathery orange and neon yellow–striped leaves against a dark green background? But then it begins to strip. Before you know it, your botanical gypsy is naked, and it is not a pretty sight.

I had ruled out the typical codiaeum for infractions far more offensive than the fact that it strings along too many vowels in its name. You can adopt the average croton for a couple of months. But before its first winter is over, *Codiaeum variegatum* var. *pictum* is generally headed for wherever you send your deflowered houseplants, thanks to its stubborn refusal to remain clothed in the average home's lack of humidity.

Then I met another croton, and it was a game changer. Not only is *Codiaeum variegatum* 'Revolutions' adorably dwarf, but it is also densely clad in long, pencil-thin leaves spangled with an irregular twinkling of star-like markings; what really clinches the deal are the curlicues that those leaves assume. No two leaves are alike, and they arrange themselves into a delightful display of squiggles that will stop traffic as people move through your home. You might want to let it preside over the living room. The curly leaves echo the legs of tables and the arms of chairs and sofas. Give it a container that accentuates its exotic side. No matter where you put it (except maybe a north-facing window), 'Revolutions' won't fail you. This new croton grows slowly, endures low light, and is generally totally durable, and it keeps its leaves intact.

Of course, you will want to reinforce the plant's tendency to remain clothed. Do not commit the transgression of overzealous watering. On the other hand, if you totally neglect to water for a protracted period of time, like weeks, it will shed a leaf or two in protest. But in general, the leaves adhere under normal circumstances. The result is pretty wow.

For the tightest package of twisted glamour, keep your croton at a respectful distance from an east- or west-facing window. Don't give it a front row seat in a sunny window, as a heavy dose of bright light will scorch the leaves. But don't be too cruel, either. A north-facing window will cause growth to stretch. That said, crotons are never going to win a growth-spurt competition. Half a year from now, chances are that your croton will look exactly the same as it did at point of purchase. This is a consolation for those who love the status quo. But consider buying a plant with about three cuttings potted together, lest 'Revolutions' appears spindly. It has so much potential.

CROTON

Codiaeum variegatum 'Revolutions'

ALSO CALLED 'Revolutions' croton
EASY

SIZE	About 12 inches (30 cm) high
FOLIAGE	Curly pencil-thin leaves, like ram's horns speckled with gold
OTHER ATTRIBUTES	Isn't that enough?
EXPOSURE	East or west
WATER REQUIREMENTS	Allow soil to dry out slightly between waterings
OPTIMUM NIGHTTIME TEMPERATURE	55–70°F (12–21°C)
RATE OF GROWTH	Very slow
SOIL TYPE	Humusy potting soil with compost included
FERTILIZING	Early spring to late autumn
ISSUES	Can lose some bottom leaves, but usually remains clad
COMPANIONS	Aglaonemas, dracaenas, ficus, ivies, peperomias, and slipper orchids

Play with your plants. Given colorful containers, *Codiaeum variegatum* 'Revolutions' is even more eye-catching.

DRACAENA

No wonder it stops traffic. With those neon leaves, who can pass *Dracaena deremensis* 'Lemon Lime' without doing a double take?

never thought I'd be dodging compliments for my dracaena. In the past, when I was ticking off must-haves for my windowsill, a dracaena might be the last suspect that came to mind. But that was before I met *Dracaena deremensis* 'Lemon Lime'.

It sort of snuck up on me, because 'Lemon Lime' was introduced when I wasn't looking. But when we found each other, it was love at first sight. With a graceful fountain of tidy leaves bordered by an astonishingly vibrant strip of almost-neon yellow against inner stripes of cream and pale green, this dracaena looks more like a designer pillow than a houseplant. Mine is always buttoned down without a sprig out of place. The gracefully wavy leaves line up and down the stem like cadets in the military. They could easily pass inspection by the top brass, and they just hold that pose in suspended animation. This plant would settle right into an updated classic decor, but its youthfully fresh color pageant could also do justice to a retro chic

country backdrop. Not many plants work in a contemporary house, but 'Lemon Lime' is the ideal candidate, especially if your palette tends toward primary shades and neon hues. Stand it beside a blue bloomer like an African violet and it smiles. Go one step further and pair it with chartreuse selaginella moss for a good-natured glow. Wherever you put it, expect it to remain constant. This dracaena does not jump through hoops, but it is best left in limbo. You can't improve perfection.

Not all dracaenas are equally shipshape. Indeed, the Internet is littered with graphic images of pathetic dracaenas that have grown far too lanky with brown leaves left intact. Don't go that route. I've had mine for three years or more, and it still hasn't reached 12 inches (30 cm) in height. I keep its roots crammed into a tight, shallow container of less than 6 inches (15 cm) in diameter. I water it, but not to excess. I don't push it. As mentioned, the status quo is fine with me.

I am frugal by nature,

so I originally purchased a single plant rather than a threesome tucked into one larger pot. For once, parsimony paid back. The combined unit does not have the impact of my single statement. When grown alone, each leaf becomes wider and the plant makes a sharper image.

Eventually the plant will need cutting back. Dracaenas are not self-branching by nature, so when they start to get leggy, step in with a pair of pruning shears. The top can be rooted in moist soil, and the lower stub should send out branches eventually. Leaving nothing more than 6 inches (15 cm) of stub is the trick to achieving a plant that might go on to win another beauty pageant. No houseplant is worth hosting unless it looks ravishing. Leaving a tall, denuded stem is not going to make anyone proud. So gather up your courage and whack it back severely.

Meanwhile, if the lower leaves brown, remove them before they mar the overall package. My dracaena has continued to retain all its leaves. Toward that goal, I water it regularly but not slavishly, as dracaenas do not appreciate being fussed over with the watering can. Preferred temperatures are usually filed in the warmth-loving category, but mine endures those 55°F (12°C) nights for which I am famous. As far as light goes, 'Lemon Lime' shows good color at a respectful distance from an east- or west-facing window; there is no need to give it the best seat in the house.

There are other dracaenas around, but they don't send me into the palpitations I have come to expect from 'Lemon Lime'. The fact that friends arrive at my door and are drawn magnetically to 'Lemon Lime' has raised the bar for the entire clan of houseplants. If guests do not instantly erupt into effusive compliments when coming in contact with a houseplant, why bother?

DRACAENA
Dracaena
EASIEST

SIZE	About 12 inches (30 cm) high, but can stretch much taller with age
FOLIAGE	Wonderful bands of neon green and forest with cream
OTHER ATTRIBUTES	It does absolutely nothing but look predictably fab, which works for me
EXPOSURE	East or west
WATER REQUIREMENTS	Allow soil to dry out slightly between waterings
OPTIMUM NIGHTTIME TEMPERATURE	60–70°F (15–21°C)
RATE OF GROWTH	Slow
SOIL TYPE	Humusy potting soil with compost included
FERTILIZING	Early spring to late autumn
ISSUES	Can grow tall without branching; lower leaves can brown
COMPANIONS	African violets, aglaonemas, begonias, crotons, ferns, ficus, ivies, mosses, and peperomias

EUPHORBIA

Firesticks (*Euphorbia tirucalli* 'Rosea') tends to look like someone stuffed some pencils into a pot. It helps to underplant it with something, like these two succulents: echeveria (similar to aloe) and *Callisia navicularis* (a succulent in the tradescantia family).

EUPHORBIA

Euphorbia

ALSO CALLED sticks-on-fire, firesticks, bishop's cap, Medusa's head

EASIEST

SIZE	Ranging from less than 1 inch to 36 inches (1 to 91 cm) high
FOLIAGE	Succulents that run the gamut; this family has some astonishing weirdos
OTHER ATTRIBUTES	Flower bracts can also be colorful
EXPOSURE	South is optimal for almost all; west is second choice
WATER REQUIREMENTS	Allow soil to dry out between waterings
OPTIMUM NIGHTTIME TEMPERATURE	50–70°F (10–21°C)
RATE OF GROWTH	Varies; usually medium
SOIL TYPE	Humusy potting soil with sand and compost included
FERTILIZING	Early spring to late autumn
ISSUES	When bruised it produces latex, which is toxic for people and pets
COMPANIONS	Agaves, aloes, geraniums, rhipsalis, senecios, and succulents

In the ever-expanding arena of ironclads, euphorbias are the clowns. Although I hope I'm convincing you that indestructible does not mean drab, the category does include a lot of corner stuffers. Many indestructibles were sleepers that got a jazzy makeover before they hit it big. But euphorbias needed no face-lift whatsoever. They are natural-born oddballs to begin with, so no further bells and whistles were necessary.

Even if you've hardly ever tackled a houseplant, you have probably had a brush with a euphorbia. Anyone who was ever saddled with a poinsettia (*Euphorbia pulcherrima*) has hosted a euphorbia. But don't let the unfortunate after-effects of poinsettias sour you on the whole tribe. Although poinsettias might be one of the flashiest members of the genus and certainly the most commercial, that cash cow is probably the least likely plant ever to survive in the average home over the long haul without inviting all manner of pests to join the party. Skip poinsettias. Or enjoy them for the few weeks before the holidays, and then wave good-bye. They are the antithesis of indestructible.

Let's move along to much better roommates to abide with after the poinsettia has been escorted to the compost heap. Plenty of euphorbias are equally outlandish, and they are ready, willing, and able to cohabitate with you. This group of plants takes kinky to another level. That can be interpreted literally, as many stand bolt upright like pokers, furnishing a room with a very exotic vertical element. Other euphorbias do contortions. I've peered through office windows to see them from the street, then told everyone nearby that someone cool was employed therein.

Because the euphorbia group is so jam-packed with weirdos,

compartmentalizing them might come in handy. I divide them into euphorbias with weapons and pacifist euphorbias. In the artillery brandishing realm, some highlights include *Euphorbia grandicornis* (aka big-horned euphorbia; those so-called horns are nasty barbs jutting from the ribs of a four-cornered stem that undulates in and out like rickrack), *E. mammillaris* (this one looks like a hybrid between a barbaric torture device and a corncob), and *E. milii* (aka crown of thorns—the nickname says it all). Each is what we used to call a conversation starter. Not everyone would describe these euphorbias as handsome, but most would agree to call them "different." In the majority of cases, blossoms are not the hallmark. *Euphorbia milii* is an exception. Not only does it have those woody stems blistered with thorns, but barberry-like leaves are also part of the picture, and speckled

versions are the new rage. In addition to all those perks, the flower bracts are stunning. Red used to be their color of choice, but as of this writing they come in pink, peach, creamy yellow, and white, as well as bicolored versions.

Einstein and I sympathize with indoor gardeners who prefer to steer clear of thorny plants. Being all paws and not a whole lot of grace when it comes to pussyfooting around houseplants, Einstein gets it. He has had a few potentially ugly encounters with crown of thorns, and it now sits where he cannot send it flying. Unarmed euphorbias include the newly popular *Euphorbia tirucalli* 'Sticks on Fire', *E. lactea* (the crested form with cockscomb-like headdresses is particularly riveting), and *E. obesa* (which looks like someone potted the baseball). All are equally indestructible except *E. obesa*, which can rot if given too much water (or normal

watering, by any other plant's standards).

A word of caution: All euphorbias produce milky lactose that bleeds from the stem when it is cut or nicked. In many cases, stems seem to break easily—well, that's what Einstein and I have found, but we vie with one another for the clod title. They are toxic and should be kept away from children and pets. Because the poinsettia industry has covered this issue ad nauseam, I will hold my peace about toxicity. As for cultivation, treat all the euphorbias mentioned as you would a succulent. Give them plenty of good light, water them sparingly (but do not allow them to go bone dry), and house them in containers that are snug rather than generous. Beyond that, you're home free with a plant that just might compete for attention with your nephew's iPhone.

TACTICS FOR DISSUADING PETS

If your cat is much worse than Einstein when it comes to kibitzing with the houseplants, you're likely at wit's end. As I've mentioned several times, many indestructible plants are toxic to pets. For more information, go to aspca.org and check out the lists of toxic plants. But note that these lists are arranged by common names, which can be confusing, and they are by no means complete. For the safety of your pets and family, please assume that no houseplant is meant to be eaten.

If you want to host a houseplant and you've got a furry nibbler in residence, you might consider researching toxicity and steering away from poisonous plants. If you have a cat like Einstein, who pesters plants but doesn't nibble, take the safe route and keep toxic plants segregated from your critter. There are several methods of keeping plants away from pets. First, do not place plants on the floor. Most pets consider ground level to be their turf. Instead, elevate plants. Sit them on top of plant stands that are tall and inaccessible. If your cat is like Einstein (who is incredibly smart—except about gravity), place the stand where your pet cannot access it by leaping via nearby furniture. For obvious reasons, don't make the destination alluring. Another method is to cluster several plants together so it is difficult to gain access

to individuals. Give your furry friend his own place in the sun where he cannot run amok. Einstein has his own perches.

Toxicity isn't the only issue. Some pets paw around in the soil of a large container. Indoor gardeners sometimes use crisscrossed tape to prevent this sort of behavior. But there's nothing beautiful about that method. Instead, you might cover your soil with river stones or some other top-dressing that pets won't find appealing. I often use ornamental orbs and pinecones for this purpose—not because Einstein is a digger, but to enhance the plant. However, the strategy might work as a deterrent.

In my experience, scented oil sprays are not effective dissuasion tactics. In fact, they have marred some of my plant leaves. Be leery. In Einstein's case, spraying him with a jet of water when I was teaching him was totally ineffective. Maine coon cats love water. Or at least, mine loves it.

And, of course, use the relationship you've built with the animal to convey your horror when something bad happens, like a toppled plant. Einstein hates histrionics. Raising the decibel level of my voice works like a charm. But if you have a pet who is an ingester, safety should come first. Don't take chances.

EVOLVULUS

Doesn't *Evolvulus glomeratus* 'Blue Daze' look like someone shrank the morning glory? It's in the same family.

Let's begin with the fact that the fraternity of indestructible plants does not abound with little blue flowers. Actually, that elusive color is fairly rare in the plant world in general, of which diehard houseplants comprise an extremely elite subset. Perhaps that's what led me to experiment with evolvulus as a houseplant in the first place. Or maybe it was autumn and I just couldn't toss the little guy out. For whatever reason, I was prepared to enter into servitude to the plant, if need be. Fortunately, it wasn't necessary—not even close.

I began by dividing *Evolvulus glomeratus* 'Blue Daze' from the combination planter where it spent the summer. I gave it a deep terra-cotta long tom container with plenty of root room, and I kept my fingers crossed. It hesitated briefly, and there was an awkward juncture when it threatened to withhold its sky blue charms. But after the trial period, it decided that life in my sunniest indoor venue wasn't so bad. It threw its energies into flower-producing mode, and soon it was like hosting a tiny morning glory (which is exactly what it is) in my window. The fact that this happened during one of the most dreadful winters on record added to my appreciation immeasurably. Those periwinkle blue flowers got a hero's welcome.

Evolvulus offers beautiful payback: a shock of long, wavy lax branches clad in furry leaves about the size of a child's thumbnail. At their tips are multiple buds that unfurl into button-size blue blossoms. It's a cheerful unit.

Is evolvulus actually carefree? No. It can get whitefly and aphids, unlike some of the more bulletproof plants in this book. But the plant falls prey to pest problems only if you stress it by causing it to wilt. If you keep it from wilting, these issues are avoidable. But it is a thirsty plant.

In addition, also unlike some of the more flexible plants in this book, you need a sunny window to enjoy blossoms on an evolvulus. I grow mine in a bright east-facing window in winter and turn it outside for a vacation in summer. And I use evolvulus as a little representation of summer's glory when you'd least expect it. Although you might avoid the hackneyed blue-and-red combination in summer containers, it's a breath of fresh air in winter. And any trailing plant with blossoms is going to stop traffic. How about growing it in your kitchen near your blue-and-white ware? Kitchens tend to be sunny, which should play in your favor. Or let it reside wherever the sun shines in to make the space feel bouncy. Evolvulus is not the easiest plant in the flock, but its pleasures are major.

EVOLVULUS
Evolvulus glomeratus

ALSO CALLED **blue daze**
EASY

SIZE	Trails down
FOLIAGE	Furry leaves, with a grayish cast, about the size of your fingernail
OTHER ATTRIBUTES	Produces periwinkle blue blossoms even in the dead of winter
EXPOSURE	Preferably south; east or west also work
WATER REQUIREMENTS	Fairly thirsty; do not allow it to wilt
OPTIMUM NIGHTTIME TEMPERATURE	50–60°F (10–15°C)
RATE OF GROWTH	Fast
SOIL TYPE	Rich, heavy potting soil with compost included
FERTILIZING	Early spring to late autumn
ISSUES	Whitefly and aphids can be a problem
COMPANIONS	Any succulent can grow alongside; in a container, try coupling it with plectranthus or rhipsalis

FERNS

A blue enamel pan cradles footed fern, *Humata tyermanii*, together with *Asplenium* 'Austral Gem' and spike moss.

Where would I be without ferns? In the initiative to cover my world with green, ferns are indispensible. As I pad around the house in the morning, eyes half open, a squirrel's foot fern frond swats me in the thigh from a nook where nothing else will grow. When I reach over to open my bedroom window at night before slipping into bed, a polypodium gently brushes against my nightgown sleeve, punctuating the end of a long day being touched by plants. If I had only a few plants clustered around the optimal windows, I would not get the full green-immersion effect. So some need to stand back from the panes in the shadows. As volunteers to take up the rear, ferns are willing and able.

Many of the indestructibles in this book have a sedate presence. They keep to themselves and form tidy packages. The ferns are a refreshing exception. They are the frothing, gangly freethinkers of the plant world, and they seem to spend most of their time dreaming up stunts beyond your ordinary botanical bag of tricks.

Ferns are quirky, and Einstein and I love oddballs. Furry feet, colorful crosiers, strange fronds, weird silhouettes—anyone who says ferns are boring is just not paying attention. They are riveting on a truly intellectual level. They are the thinking person's no-brainer. That sounds like an oxymoron, but you want a green roommate with substance. Highly refined should not equal high maintenance.

Maybe you have steered clear of ferns because they seem like divas. You assume anything that looks exceptionally good is bound to require hair and makeup. Fortunately, that isn't the case with most ferns. Some have a bad rap for being snobby about humidity, but I avoid those types. The fact that most of my oldest houseplants are ferns is telling. Just like you, I occasionally forget to water. For that reason, I have given up on maidenhairs (*Adiantum* species) heart fern (*Hemionitis arifolia*), and most Boston

or sword ferns (*Nephrolepis exaltata* and *Nephrolepis cordifolia*, the exception being miniature *Nephrolepis cordifolia* 'Duffii', which is delightfully bulletproof). Or, to be more accurate, those types have given up on me. But what remains is a vast field of blissfully house-appropriate beauties that fill spaces where other, more light-gluttonous plants might refuse to grow. When only the brave are left standing, you still have some dazzlers in the brew.

Indestructible ferns are majestic, regal, gracious, and glorious, not booby prizes. Grown well, a fern fills its niche with panache. If given

Beside the blue enamelware, a white colander spills over with various mosses, which make great companions for ferns. Both dwell on the far side of the bathroom, away from the windows.

the right presentation, a fern will step out of the shadows and be every bit as wow-worthy as any bloomer. It's all in the coupling of plant with container, and I spend a lot of time fussing over that merger. Appropriately displayed ferns make the leap from a house where everything is clustered around the windowsills to a place where green is pretty much everywhere you look. But even ferns require the occasional rotation to keep from arching toward the light source, especially when I push the limits and position them where light is really low. But I try not to do that on a regular basis because they deserve better. Don't grow a plant if you can't help it become its best self. Plants have pride too.

The Victorians made ferneries, both outdoors and inside. I find the concept enthralling. Ferns make very handsome companions for fellow ferns. There is so much diversity in frond textures and hues that the collection comes off as truly sophisticated and artistically enthralling. Taking this concept one step further, I sometimes tuck ferns into mutual planters and let their fronds interweave into a tapestry of texture. It reads like a dell indoors. And because ferns do not demand high beams, I can put my creations into the middle of a room to disperse the natural motif beyond being merely tied to the windows.

You are probably worried about humidity, and I don't blame you—it can be an issue for ferns. My home is not particularly dry. Petting Einstein never produces sparks, and lizard skin isn't an issue for me. But it's not a sauna in here, either. Many ferns dwell in the bathroom, where I spend far too much time singing in the shower (hopefully they are equally tone-deaf). But ferns are not confined to that space; they live just about everywhere except the brightest windows. If your home has a dry atmosphere, consider running a humidifier. Everyone will benefit and be grateful, including the green occupants.

Containers are key. If you give a fern ample root room,

FERNS

Asplenium, Athyrium, Davallia, Humata, Nephrolepis, Polypodium, and *Pteris*

EASY

SIZE	Ranging from 5 to 24 inches (12 to 61 cm) high, depending on the variety
FOLIAGE	Incredibly diverse—sometimes lacy but not always; gray, blue-green, and other hues available
OTHER ATTRIBUTES	Great for low-light conditions; some have furry feet
EXPOSURE	East or west; north is also possible
WATER REQUIREMENTS	Usually thirsty; keep soil moderately moist
OPTIMUM NIGHTTIME TEMPERATURE	55–70°F (12–21°C)
RATE OF GROWTH	Medium
SOIL TYPE	Rich, humusy, peaty potting soil with compost included
FERTILIZING	Early spring to late autumn
ISSUES	Can be pestered by scale; steer away from the Boston and sword ferns as well as maidenhairs, which are fussy
COMPANIONS	Try making combination planters with several diverse ferns; begonias, dracaenas, ivies, peperomias, and philodendrons also coexist

most of your problems will be solved. Many ferns rapidly make extensive roots to slurp up moisture. In a shallow or cramped pot, the roots dry out frequently, which leads to problems. On the other hand, don't overdo it. The root system shouldn't swim in its container. And, of course, a nutritious organic potting soil is going to spell the difference between an okay-looking fern and a beauty queen.

Speaking of centerfolds, grooming is everything in the world of ferns. When they are happy, ferns produce plentiful fronds that form tresses rivaling Tina Turner's mane. But the moment a frond begins to turn pale, whisk it away. Staying on top of watering also prevents problems before they strike. Ferns prefer to be evenly moist, not sopping wet and never parched.

Ferns are prone to scale. If yours falls victim, keep in mind that ferns are sensitive to many oil-based sprays. To be sure that a spray is not going to harm your fern, first check the label. Then, just to be on the safe side, test any

treatment on a small area of the plant with a dilute application. Always spray outdoors (even if your treatment is organic) and early in the day. After treatment, keep the plant from bright light for a day or more.

Celebrate your ferns. There is no need to pamper them, but pay attention. Give them the glad hand on a regular basis. If you really *grow* your ferns, rather than just pulling them where they mark time, they will thrive and respond, waxing luxuriant. With their woodsy mood and outdoorsy connection, ferns deliver memories of rural hikes and other outward-bound excursions right into the heart of your home. They will shower your life with euphoria.

This hollowed-out log holding a group of mosses and ferns feels like you just stumbled upon it in the woods.

GOT DARK SHADOWS?

It should surprise no one to learn that Michael Trapp sleeps with ferns. The fact that an immense polypodium has settled into one corner of his bedroom, growing more corpulent over the years, will not shock anyone who knows the interior designer and antiques dealer. Although I wouldn't really call Michael the King of Noir, he does have his dark side. It stands to reason that he pals around with anything that lurks in the shadows.

In truth, Michael's shop and home in West Cornwall, Connecticut, makes the most of available light. He took a rather forlorn house under his wing years ago. The place is decidedly somber, but only because the decor is strictly time-warped. What's actually macabre about Michael is his aesthetic. Crumbling, cracked, tarnished, and cloudy are all cool with him. He avoids new and pristine. Any plant that would be more at home in the Jurassic Period fits right in. Ferns are just the ticket.

Michael's mother grew ferns because they transitioned well to other homes and his family moved continually. When Michael finally settled into a home and shop of his own, the result was a lot of smoky Viennese glass and statuary with various limbs no longer intact. The place is like a Victorian fernery minus the frump. He designed part of the house with stone floors and heating pipes below. That wonderful combination of warmth and high humidity just delights the ferns. Indeed, Michael's ferns keep chugging along despite the fact that he makes frequent excursions collecting antiques while the ferns stay home with his cat, Mrs. Trapp. She isn't great with care and maintenance; slumber is her primary specialty. But the ferns still do quite well.

Of course, it's not all peachy keen, nor would Michael want it that way. He doesn't really mind the rivalry between Mrs. Trapp and the fern that threatens to appropriate her position in Michael's bedroom. With a stern hiss and a stiff swat, the polypodium has learned to keep its fronds to itself.

In Michael Trapp's cracked domain, *Pteris ensiformis* 'Evergemiensis' sends a wayward frond to tickle an urn on a mantel.

Lurking in a grotto,
Polypodium aureum
'Blue Star' wends
beside sea coral and
shells.

FICUS

Not all ficus plants are easy roommates. *Ficus benjamina* is the family member that most gardeners try to grow, and it is a bear. I have absolutely no luck with it. Undoubtedly you have encountered tree-size versions of *F. benjamina* in malls and corporate buildings. I figure they work with a rotating supply of understudies. For me, that ficus drops leaves pitifully and makes a total and constant mess of my home. Skip it. Even its scaled-down version, 'Too Little', is prone to do a striptease.

There are ficus that can share your home without inflicting heartache. Mistletoe fig, *Ficus deltoidea*, is an easygoing cousin to its peevish kin. It also comes from a more attractive branch of the family (of course, any plant looks better with all its leaves attached rather than totally naked). The mistletoe fig has style; its branches twist and turn around with the grace of a ballerina. Its leaves are thick and triangular in a rounded-edge sort of way. And it produces pea-size nonedible figs in profusion. Use it as a small bush to give your home the sense of shrubby architecture—no piece of furniture could possibly compare. Plus, it is amenable as well as adorable. Figs tend to be heavy drinkers, but if you are lax with the watering can, the mistletoe fig's nose doesn't get out of joint. And the foliage stays put. You might have a few yellowed leaves if it goes bone dry, but nothing more dramatic occurs.

If you like the look of *Ficus benjamina*, *F. salicifolia* is a miniature version that looks like someone shrank its cantankerous big brother. It makes a great bonsai as long as you keep it supplied with water. It will drop leaves as a result of supreme neglect, but generally it's easy. You can create a lovely scene by pairing it with mini ground covers in a combo planter.

If you need a plant that can tolerate an extremely challenging environment, like a dorm room, try the rubber tree, *Ficus elastica*. For the longest time, rubber trees were relegated to has-been status. Not surprisingly, nobody was particularly interested in adopting a plant that takes up a lot of space, has a gawky stature, tends to be a dust magnet, and sports lackluster, nondescript large leaves. Unless you were Uniroyal, *Ficus elastica* failed to impress. But that was yesterday. A few new progeny have been added to sweeten the deal, such as 'Doescheri' with pinkish and grayish leaves, and 'Tineke', which has bold variegation. They have all the tenacity of their Victorian ancestors, but far more pizzazz. These make great office plants, and they reputedly clean the air very efficiently. However, as far as I know, their bolt-upright growth habit has not changed, and they are not prone to branching out. If you want something shapely, you might have to find replacements every few years.

Then there's creeping fig. *Ficus pumila* bears no physical resemblance to any of the figs just mentioned. With twining, crawling branches and truly athletic energy, this plant just wants to roam. It throws out more arms and

Unlike the species, *Ficus pumila*, variegated 'Snowflake' minds its manners and isn't equally wayward.

legs than an octopus and grows just about anywhere. Most figs can withstand low-light situations, but creeping fig takes that tolerance to another level of durability. Got a dark closet? This plant will probably survive it. It won't look particularly presentable and it will be scantily clad, but I've seen creeping fig traveling across cellars in its quest for a light source on the other side. Give it a place where it can cover ground, and watch it go crazy. I use it as a draping plant below taller potmates such as ponytail palms. By the way, there is no need to give creeping fig a fancy container. It will camouflage its host in no time. Or, for something with a little more reserve, try *F. pumila* 'Minima', which has smaller, crinklier leaves and a slower pace. Plus, there are variegated smaller versions, like 'Snowflake', with good manners. 'Quercifolia', with its minute, oak-shaped leaves, is so slow it feels like suspended animation.

The trait that recommends most ficus as happy housemates is the fact that

Planted in a window box with polka dot plant, *Ficus pumila* 'Snowflake' shares similar markings, and the two romp happily together.

FICUS
Ficus

ALSO CALLED **fig**

EASY

SIZE	Most are upright, ranging in size from 6 inches (15 cm) to several feet high; some creep along the soil surface
FOLIAGE	Extremely varied in form; generally green
OTHER ATTRIBUTES	Often used as an indoor tree
EXPOSURE	East or west
WATER REQUIREMENTS	Keep soil moderately moist; do not allow it to dry out
OPTIMUM NIGHTTIME TEMPERATURE	50–65°F (10–18°C)
RATE OF GROWTH	Medium (faster than the speed of light for *Ficus pumila*)
SOIL TYPE	Rich, humusy potting soil with compost included
FERTILIZING	Early spring to late autumn
ISSUES	Avoid ficus that drop leaves; ficus are prone to scale and even *Ficus pumila* objects to prolonged forgetful watering
COMPANIONS	Aglaonemas, aspidistras, begonias, bromeliads, ferns, hoyas, ivies, nerve plants, peperomias, polka dot plants, ponytail palms, and scheffleras; *Ficus pumila* and its cultivars can be used as a ground cover when paired with other plants

they can endure low-light conditions with stoic fortitude. Of course, if you give them a bright east- or west-facing window, they will love you for it and will display their appreciation with tighter growth and better leaf color. And they all seem to be heavy drinkers. Leaf drop can result from neglecting to quench their thirst. As for food, I don't see a whole lot of difference between a ficus that has been fertilized regularly and one that is not fed on a regular basis. In fact, if you feed *Ficus pumila* liberally, watch out: It can take over your life.

GERANIUM

Ivy-leaf geranium, *Pelargonium peltatum* 'Sofie Cascade', is as amiable as the more common zonal geranium, but it has ivy-shaped leaves and a sprawling habit that's actually easier to host.

Something magenta is happening on the windowsill. That may not sound particularly cataclysmic, considering that my sills tend toward colorful. But it is November, and this is a singularly drab edition of late autumn. The spark of light that might kindle blossoms is conspicuously lacking. Other bloomers, like chiritas and similar members of the African violet family, are biding their time. But not the geraniums. They are totally gung ho.

I love eager things. Something about golden retrievers with their thumping tails gets me all mushy inside. Geraniums and I have always been linked. When I first started working at Logee's Greenhouses, I begged to take the geraniums under my wing (in addition to curating the begonia collection, tending the herbs, running the mail-order department, writing the catalog, and learning to use a Graflex billows camera). Actually, the Logee's folks didn't have a choice— you couldn't keep geraniums and me apart. It was like the pull of two magnets.

It's still that way. I pray there's never a winter without a geranium on my windowsill. I like the foliage. I love the smell (yes, the scented-leaved geraniums are a hoot, but plain old ordinary zonal geraniums also have a signature fragrance). However, the flowers really do it for me. They come in outrageously retro shades that are unabashedly zippy. Beyond even the varsity shades, these colors are psychedelic. They don't make hues like these anymore.

I'm referring, of course, to pelargoniums. They are in the Geraniaceae, but are actually kissing cousins of true geraniums, the type you grow as perennials outdoors. These tender versions were welcomed indoors among the earliest houseplants, which says a lot about their fortitude. My aunt-in-law, Mary Ellen Ross, who founded Merryspring Nature Center in Camden, Maine, claims to have coined the saying, "Geraniums ask so little, but give so much." She grew them for decades. Late one afternoon in midwinter

Fancy leaf heirloom *Pelargonium* 'A Happy Thought' has variegated leaves and bright red flowers in its bag of tricks.

when I was watering the geraniums, she yanked the hose out of my hands and bellowed, "You're not watering these late in the day, are you?" I assured her I was not. And I never did it again.

That might be the only concession I make to geraniums. I water sparingly and only early in the day. Geraniums tell you when they've been stressed by thirst. Their lower leaves turn yellow and then brown while the upper leaves remain gloriously green. If you make amends immediately, no further browning occurs. Thanks to Aunt Mary Ellen, I've also learned to keep water off the foliage. Aside from that, it's pretty much a steady diet of leaving them alone and watching the performance. And I'm talking about serious hands off. I rarely repot them and I fertilize only in high summer. I do, however, practice all my pruning skills on their stems. Geraniums love to be pruned. You can scarcely go wrong. The more you clip away, the more gratefully they branch. Periodic stern shearings spur revitalization. Be sure to clip back to a place where new

growth is shooting from the side of the stem. Geraniums are prone to so-called blind eyes, junctures where no growth is emerging to result in branching.

In the geranium arena, you have plenty of options. For me, it is neck and neck whether I prefer the regular zonal types or the scented-leaf species. You have to love a plant that goes around smelling like Old Spice. Furthermore, you can select among nutmeg, ginger, lime, pine, peppermint, and innumerable others. Scented-leaf geraniums follow the same lines as herbs, and they could fill the same niche in your home. I find the tiny-leaved lemon crispum types to be a little dicey (especially the variegated 'Prince Rubert'), so you might avoid them. Most of the scented types do not have flowers that equal the shades of the zonals, but some of the rose-scented cultivars come close. Other easy geraniums include ivy-leaf types (nonvariegated versions tend to be the most amiable) that sprawl and branch willingly rather than jut straight upward.

If your geranium fails to

blossom, you probably over-potted it or furnished too much food. I find that they blossom even when light levels are low. Of course, if you can provide a south-facing window, more power (and blossoms) to you. But east or west will suffice.

As for display of the zonal geraniums, you could go in any direction you wish. Give them an old English flowerpot à la Guy Wolff and they'll look like they came from Rembrandt Peale's own collection. They fit in beautifully with a colonial home. Or opt for something sleek and keep them heavily pruned, and their spectrum can match a disco ball. Wherever and however you show them off, what we really love about geraniums is their reliability. Their performance in summer is legendary. Geraniums were once spread throughout every cemetery in the country come Memorial Day. But in the depths of winter, when you really need magenta, they burst out with a big smooch of color. Sure, tell everyone you earned those blossoms. But in truth, it was a cakewalk.

GERANIUM
Pelargonium

ALSO CALLED **zonal geranium, scented-leaf geranium**
EASIEST

SIZE	Ranging from 8 to 24 inches (20 to 61 cm) high
FOLIAGE	For zonal geraniums, usually rounded green with a horse-shoe mark, but chartreuse fancy-leaf versions are popular; scented geraniums are more diverse
OTHER ATTRIBUTES	Produces colorful blossoms all year, including in the dead of winter
EXPOSURE	South, east, or west
WATER REQUIREMENTS	Keep soil moderately moist; aim to water the soil rather than the foliage
OPTIMUM NIGHTTIME TEMPERATURE	50–60°F (10–15°C)
RATE OF GROWTH	Medium to fast
SOIL TYPE	Rich, heavy potting soil with compost included
FERTILIZING	Early spring to late autumn
ISSUES	Pruning is necessary to encourage branching; whitefly can be a problem
COMPANIONS	A display of many geraniums is glorious, or go with iresine, plectranthus, rhipsalis, and succulents

COLORFUL CHARACTERS

Geraniums were not necessarily a natural for Lee Link. While she was growing up in the 1960s, her mother cultivated them. But Lee's personal style evolved more toward the exotic and obscure, with an international twist and a cosmopolitan savvy. She pooh-poohed them for a while. "I became rather snooty about geraniums," she admits. But long ago Lee got over any attitude she felt toward pelargoniums. How did they redeem themselves? Easy. "They just keep flowering and flowering," she marvels. It's hard not to like something so congenial.

In all other aspects of her life, Lee tends to keep things fairly streamlined. So she can be forgiven for a little indulgence when it comes to plants, an infatuation that has necessitated at least two additions to the A-frame she and her husband, Fritz, bought in the Berkshire foothills ages ago.

Meanwhile, Lee was branching out beyond the usual zonal geranium realm. She caught wind of the species geraniums, and they were just the ticket for someone fond of kinky but also keen on blossoms. The unusual detail that they go dormant in summer and grow in the winter also gives her secret glee. "I'll probably be the only person who sees them, but that works for me."

Meanwhile, she still grows plenty of old faithfuls—lots of standard-issue magenta geraniums that might be comfortable in a cemetery urn share her hospitality. But she parts company with the rank and file in her presentation. Her containers run the gamut, and each one is a work of art. As soon as a plant comes into her jurisdiction, it becomes a runway model. Creative container combos are not the only area where makeovers are manifest. Lee's plants get hair and makeup treatments regularly: "I prune the bejeezus out of them." She also takes cuttings and makes more geraniums, which has caused something of a population explosion. "I have to stop doing that," she admits. "It's just sheer madness." But who can blame her?

For their variegated foliage and fragrant leaves, Lee grows rose-scented geraniums like *Pelargonium* 'Lady Plymouth' and *P.* 'Frosted'.

You are apt to encounter plants and botanical oddities just about everywhere in Lee's home, and vignettes with geraniums, like dwarf *Pelargonium* 'Snow White', are common.

Called zebra plant because of the barnacle-like encrustations on its leaves, *Haworthia fasciata* goes way back as a houseplant.

I never doubted that *Haworthia fasciata* was indestructible. Actually, I didn't think much about it one way or another until I dragged home a couple of zebra plants from a nursery and then forgot about them for an embarrassingly lengthy juncture. Exactly how long they were in purgatory, I won't confess. But the end result following this prolonged period of abuse was not a whole lot different than the outcome after two months of TLC.

Then I had an even more dramatic brush with the plant and its fortitude. At the Philadelphia Flower Show, a vendor was selling a little shadowbox unit with two *Haworthia fasciata* plants glued in. They had some sphagnum moss tucked around their base, but the presentation was akin to asking a few plants to totter on the brink of a cliff for an indefinite interlude. I hung the box in good light and water the haworthias periodically, but it's certainly life on the edge. And yet the plants are doing just fine.

The way I see it, any plant that endured our grandmothers' generation to become a standby in homes had to boast a lion's share of courage. Although I'm sure some grandmothers had infinite expendable time, mine definitely did not. *Haworthia fasciata* was a fixture in their day. It isn't quite as prevalent today, but you can still find this plant wherever people want something zany but don't want to fret over it.

What you shouldn't expect from this haworthia, or any of them, is excitement. I find them exceptionally attractive, but they don't do stunts. They don't die, but they don't really perform, either. They just sit there in suspended animation with their deep green pointy rosettes studded with white barnacle-like encrustations all around. They look like something you might pull from a shipwreck. It's a little kinky, but it appeals to a certain crowd (including me).

As far as care goes, haworthias need almost none. For the best color and tightness, give them a bright window if you can. But if you cannot whip up radiant light, it's

HAWORTHIA
Haworthia fasciata

ALSO CALLED **zebra plant**
EASIEST

SIZE	3 inches (7 cm) high
FOLIAGE	Succulent, pointed, dark green, aloe-like stems with white encrustations running horizontally
OTHER ATTRIBUTES	Tolerates near-death experiences
EXPOSURE	South is optimal; west is second choice
WATER REQUIREMENTS	Allow soil to dry out between waterings
OPTIMUM NIGHTTIME TEMPERATURE	50–70°F (10–21°C)
RATE OF GROWTH	Very slow
SOIL TYPE	Humusy potting soil with sand and compost included
FERTILIZING	Unnecessary
ISSUES	None, except suspended animation is the status quo
COMPANIONS	Agaves, aloes, euphorbias, rhipsalis, senecios, and succulents

okay. You might end up with a plant that is not as bolt upright as its directly lit kin, but that will be the worst of your consequences. *Haworthia fasciata* does not require much water. In fact, overdoing it might be the plant's undoing. But sprinkle it when the soil is dry and it will be immensely grateful.

Haworthia fasciata is the most amiable and readily available of a group of plants that are collectors' items. Many of the other haworthias have wonderful, window-like leaves and bizarre forms. They are not particularly difficult plants, but they can get browned foliage if you over-water or splash the leaves. *Haworthia fasciata* is the easiest of the batch.

HENS AND CHICKS

From a distance, these hens and chicks might look all the same. But when you examine them closely, *Sempervivum arachnoideum*, S. 'Mrs. Giuseppi', and S. 'Oddity' are very different.

've already confessed to being a clod. I wouldn't exactly describe myself as a buffoon, but I do commit my fair share of blunders. Most of the time they result in broken pots or similar disasters, but sometimes being a klutz leads to some cool discoveries, like finding the houseplant in hens and chicks.

If I had planted a certain sempervivum in the garden in a timely fashion while the growing season was still under way, I never would have known what a good roommate hens and chicks can become. It's sort of like discovering that the shy guy in the corner of the classroom plays a mean saxophone.

I'm a sucker for an autumn sale. I swoop into a garden center with no intention of adopting anything ("Just to check out what's left"). In two blinks of an eye, the back of my station wagon is full. Some of it gets in the ground before hard frost, and some doesn't. Hens and chicks missed the boat. While feeling contrite, I gave it a snazzy container,

but I didn't lend it prime real estate in the window. The best seats are assigned on a first-come-first-served basis, so hens and chicks didn't even get the balcony. They were stuffed in a nearly forgotten corner. This might have been lethal for a less stalwart individual, but the plant was not fazed.

I know you've seen hens and chicks somewhere. Sempervivums are little ground covers that make rosettes in the garden and sprout a clutch of smaller rosettes clustered around. Your cat digs them up and tosses them about, but they still send out new roots. The ground bakes, no problem. The mower shoots lawn clippings in their faces, and they turn the other cheek. If there ever was a plant that might survive your hot-air vent inside, sempervivum is a good candidate.

At a lecture I gave recently, someone in the audience raised her hand timidly. She was growing a hens and chicks, but something frightening was occurring. "The middle of the plant is sort of erupting," she said in a

shaky voice. I knew exactly what she meant because the same thing was happening to mine. "Congratulations!" I answered. "It's blooming, and you're the proud mama." You should have seen her face light up with a smile.

I admit, the little Vesuvius that hens and chicks send up in preparation for flowering can be slightly disconcerting. To novice eyes, it could resemble doom. Suddenly, the rosette starts to jut upward. You begin to worry that the poor thing is craving the light you haven't delivered. Fortunately, the eruption doesn't leave you guessing for long; instead it begins to develop promising buds. From there, star-shaped flowers follow fairly rapidly. Depending on the variety, they're usually peach-pink or tinted cream. They linger and look great. No matter where you stashed your sempervivum off the beaten track originally, it gets pulled front and center when the flowers form in late winter or early spring. Your pride swells.

Besides the blooming fanfare, hens and chicks are

probably not going to be much more than supporting actors. If you scoop up a lot of them to pot together, they make a nice presentation. I like to display them in an urn-shaped container on the sidelines of the room—near a window, if possible. They could also grow below another plant as an indoor ground cover for a plant with a naked stem or maybe a ponytail palm. Potting one variety solo is handsome, but combining several different types can lead to a mosaic-like presentation. The subtle diversity of this plant in its many guises with different colored foliage is riveting, in a plantoholic sort of way. There's even one that looks like spiderwebs have been strung between the leaves.

No matter how you use a sempervivum, it's probably going to survive. If you give it a south-facing window, the rosettes will snuggle together tightly and the plant will shine. In an east- or west-facing window, or pulled away from the light source, the plant will not be such a compact nugget. But it never looks untidy.

The same goes for watering: Although drenching the plant isn't a great idea for its long-term health, it usually tolerates underwatering. In fact, you can be downright forgetful and hens and chicks is fine. Temperatures can run the gamut. Sempervivums are hardy perennials, so you can grow them on that barely heated porch without fear of repercussions. Too hot is equally simpatico; after all, this is a succulent. I do have one problem with hens and chicks: root mealybug. They find this plant irresistible. I now check the root system at the nursery by turning the plant upside down and examining it for tiny white flecks around the root ball. When in doubt, reject the plant. Root mealybug is not easily cured by organic methods, and it can spread like wildfire. Other than that, sempervivums are a dream come true for clods and ultra-coordinated indoor gardeners alike.

HENS AND CHICKS
Sempervivum
ALSO CALLED **house leek**
EASIEST

SIZE	Creeps along the ground
FOLIAGE	Succulent, rosettes (hens) surrounded by smaller rosettes (chicks) in a variety of colors
OTHER ATTRIBUTES	Erupts into a spire of star-like blossoms
EXPOSURE	South is optimal for almost all; west is second choice
WATER REQUIREMENTS	Allow soil to dry out between waterings
OPTIMUM NIGHTTIME TEMPERATURE	45–70°F (7–21°C)
RATE OF GROWTH	Slow
SOIL TYPE	Humusy potting soil with sand and compost included
FERTILIZING	Unnecessary
ISSUES	Prone to root mealybug
COMPANIONS	Agaves, aloes, rhipsalis, senecios, and other succulents

HOYA

I keep hoyas in my bedroom window all year long because I simply cannot live without them. *Hoya carnosa* (far left) is an heirloom variety, but *H. compacta* (in the urn) is a more interesting version.

When I open my eyes in the morning, no matter what the hour, Einstein is patrolling the bedroom window and surveying the dawn maneuvers in the backyard. By the time I get out there, the deer prancing and skunk waltzing have broken up for the day. Einstein won't reveal what transpired, even though he witnessed all the dirty deeds from his perch. At one time, I had a plant on the pedestal right in front of his favorite bedroom window. That strategic position is now dedicated to his front-and-center surveillance missions. The hoya and fern have to stand aside.

Even though it was displaced, the hoya is happy taking a backseat. In fact, a full-frontal east-facing window might be a little too much for its complexion at certain times of year. Hoyas can easily sunburn— that's their only caveat. This explains why *Hoya compacta* keeps a permanent position in my bedroom and doesn't go outside with the rest of the summer sojourners. But

the hoya's dislike of sunrays is only one facet of the justification. This plant is so swank that waking up would not be the same without it. And hoyas require absolutely no maintenance, which is another good reason to recommend the plant for a perpetual, very visible position.

Like most gardeners, I launch out of bed fairly quickly after waking. But in bad weather I take a few minutes to enjoy the surrounding scenery and soak up the vibes from the glass cloche beside my bed and the houseplants in the window. First impressions are everything, and the hoya is impeccably dressed no matter what the season. Yes, it is a contortionist. But I love kinky. I do yoga; the hoya does yoga.

Once I'm up and running, there's no looking back. If the bed doesn't get smoothed out and the pillows aren't plumped immediately, chances are they'll be forgotten in the mad rush. The hoya doesn't always get watered. Despite the fact that its root system is wedged into an urn that it

probably outgrew ages ago (but looks so chic), it chugs along without batting a leaf. It never drops foliage. And the dark green (there are variegated versions), crinkly leaves form a chain, which is how it earned its nickname of Hindu rope vine.

Not only does *Hoya compacta* win the congeniality award in the genus and earn the best-dressed designation, the performance doesn't end after the first act. In spring and summer, it bursts into blossoms, a series of three concentric five-pointed stars similar to its relative the milkweed. It's a pale pink constellation within a white star within a cream-colored asterisk, just the sort of upbeat thing you need to see in the morning. Some people don't like the scent, but I adore it. It's like baby powder mixed with molasses. Granted, the blossoms shed onto the floor after the show, but not before they've appeared for a lengthy engagement.

Blossoms on hoyas result only from neglect. Fortunately, I love the container in which my *Hoya compacta*

When my wax flower blossomed, it added yet another perk to an already riveting package (plus, it's fragrant).

resides, and I'm not about to grant a graduation in the foreseeable future. That's the secret ingredient to achieving flowers. In so many instances, relatives inherit an ancient hoya that draped around their mother's or aunt's or grandmother's house and generously repot it into a larger new container. The promotion makes watering easier, but you won't see flowers for years. Lavish feeding will bring similar results, or lack thereof.

Although I have a specimen *Hoya carnosa*, I keep it only because I'm a sap for anything with history. My dog-eared *Henderson's Handbook of Plants and General Horticulture* (1890) claims it was introduced in 1802 and hails it as a steadfast survivor capable of enduring the dustiest parlor. The fact that it does nothing much but stay alive was fine with everyone back then. As for me, it is sufficient that *H. carnosa* does nothing much beyond being nostalgic. But that's only because it requires almost no care.

My variegated *Hoya kerrii* (it came from a

mom-and-pop greenhouse without a label, and these plants go under several names, including 'Albomarginata' and 'Splash') is equally cool with neglect. However, when it comes to growth, this particular hoya takes painfully slow to another level. The ultra-thick, leathery, distinctly heart-shaped leaves are extraordinarily unique, but you can spend a lifetime waiting for this plant to fill out. While you're standing by, be absolutely sure not to give it bright light, because that will scorch all the progress you've already made. Take it from a sadder-but-wiser hoya grower.

I rank *Hoya lanceolata* subsp. *bella*, *H. pubera*, and *H. lacunosa* in the more difficult category. They aren't really challenges to grow, but they are not indestructible. They seem more prone to root mealybug than the diehards, and it is not hard to sabotage them. Steer toward the old faithfuls, unless you are ready for a challenge.

Hoyas serve an important role in any home because they spill down. Have you

HOYA

Hoya

ALSO CALLED porcelain flower, wax flower, Hindu rope vine

EASIEST

SIZE	Drapes down
FOLIAGE	Usually long, thin, and leathery; *Hoya compacta* has crinkled leaves, and variegated versions are available
OTHER ATTRIBUTES	One of the few very tidy vines; the flowers are way cool and fragrant
EXPOSURE	East or west; does not like very bright light
WATER REQUIREMENTS	Keep soil moderately moist
OPTIMUM NIGHTTIME TEMPERATURE	60–70°F (15–21°C)
RATE OF GROWTH	Slow
SOIL TYPE	Rich, humusy, peaty potting soil with compost included
FERTILIZING	Early spring to late autumn
ISSUES	Can be prone to scale and mealybug; fails to blossom unless pot-bound
COMPANIONS	Begonias, ferns, ivies, nerve plants, peace lilies, peperomias, philodendrons, and pileas

noticed that most vines tend toward slightly ill-kempt behavior? Hoyas are tidy. *Hoya carnosa* is almost buttoned down, while *H. compacta* is pulled together in a strictly nontraditional sort of way. But vines introduce a display quandary for some gardeners. Hanging baskets can be hell to deal with indoors. They bop you on the head when you're attempting to shut the window. They swing around when you're trying to water, and you end up sprinkling the floor. They make whatever they are cradling the polar opposite of low maintenance. But if you use a tall container or urn rather than a hanging pot to house showering plants, all your problems are solved. Your hoya will drape majestically down, you will get a sort of peekaboo look at the container's silhouette, and you will have created an insta-matic sculpture. Not bad for a day's work.

IRESINE

If you love gawky, you're going to be crazy about beefsteak plants. Nothing is more fun than training *Iresine herbstii* 'Blazin' Rose' to flex its muscles.

Sometimes you need a clown. Other indestructibles tend to be stiff-upper-lip plants that could be the tough guy in an action film. Clad in leathery leaves, most diehards can face anything your family dishes out and still make a fierce comeback. Nobody kicks dirt in their faces, and they look the part. A beefsteak plant, on the other hand, appears to be a cream puff.

Beefsteak plants are the goofballs of the indestructible department. Anything that has earned the common name chicken gizzard must have a sense of humor. Coleus is an apt comparison. We're talking thick, succulent red stems that look more like biceps, and maroon leaves with magenta markings that resemble African tribal masks. This plant is funky. And in addition to the red prototype, there's a lime-colored version (*Iresine herbstii* 'Blazin' Lime') with medium green leaves streaked by lemon markings enhanced by a touch of magenta when new leaves sprout against the plant's signature red stems. Plus, I just found 'Purple Lady', which breaks out of the upright boilerplate formula and sprawls along horizontally with outstretched thick stems that support the crinkled wine-colored leaves without spilling over. It makes a great ground cover below other plants to disguise the soil and play up the color.

Although it might look like a softy, this plant is no pushover. Nothing gets the best of an iresine. This fact took me totally by surprise. Somehow I found one in my shopping cart (how do these things happen?) in the middle of the summer. At the time, I was continually on the road. Despite

When *Iresine herbstii* 'Blazin' Lime' started looking like an espalier, I trained it onto a trellis that just happened to fit perfectly into its pot.

GALLERY OF INDESTRUCTIBLES

the fact that my house sitters don't always remember to water, come autumn the beefsteak plant was still hanging around with a big grin. Not a leaf was missing. How could I help but bring it inside? This seemed like a great way to introduce the garden's puckish flamboyance to the indoors and keep the converted barn on the light side. I had only a north-facing window available, but this was not a problem. It got a little lanky (I treat it better now), but it soldiered on. Forgot to water. Fine. Neglected to fertilize. Never missed a beat. Skipped repotting. What, me worry?

Of course, better people than I do all of the above. But if you drop the ball, this little windowsill warrior is probably not going to suffer over the long haul. It will wilt, but not permanently. If you can do only one thing to keep your beefsteak plant happy, water it regularly. My

plants (and I have hosted several) wilted a few times, but they sprang up again, although the stems got thicker and more succulent. And they never fell victim to aphids, even under severe stress ('Purple Lady' might not be equally impervious—I'm still conducting the testing). Be warned, however: I cannot promise yours will come from equally stoic stock. If nothing else, try to remember to visit this plant with a watering can. Occasional pruning will also go a long way, because beefsteak plants can get beefy. As long as you leave some foliage, feel free to be brutal. I sort of like the lanky look. In fact, I train my beefsteak plant as an espalier so part of the glamour is the swollen stems. I have a trellis that fits perfectly in its pot, and it spreads its arms out like a benediction over the entire room. Everyone smiles.

IRESINE
Iresine

ALSO CALLED **beefsteak plant, chicken gizzard, bloodleaf**
EASY

SIZE	20 to 36 inches (50 to 91 cm) high, except sprawling 'Purple Lady'
FOLIAGE	Wine with magenta markings or lime with lemon markings
OTHER ATTRIBUTES	Bright, cheerful colored leaves
EXPOSURE	East, west, or south
WATER REQUIREMENTS	Keep soil moderately moist
OPTIMUM NIGHTTIME TEMPERATURE	50–65°F (10–18°C)
RATE OF GROWTH	Fast
SOIL TYPE	Rich, humusy potting soil with compost included
FERTILIZING	Early spring to late autumn
PROPAGATION	Easily rooted by cuttings, like coleus
ISSUES	Will wilt, but revives readily
COMPANIONS	Aglaonemas, geraniums, philodendrons, and senecios

Ivies are so prevalent in supermarkets that they rarely come with names. Einstein likes the companionship of a trailing plant, but he doesn't nibble—ivies are toxic to pets.

Ivies got me into this pickle in the first place. Granted, I was born a nature enthusiast. I always wanted plants nearby, and fairly early in the game I began to hanker for houseplants. But "children" and "responsibility" are rarely uttered in the same breath. And I was no different at the age of eight. I spent endless hours playing with my cat, but my mother probably made up for my many lapses filling her bowl with food. My mom kept her own plant menagerie—mostly philodendrons, succulents, and African violets—in the kitchen where she could monitor their progress or lack thereof (she prefers slow and steady when it comes to plants). My stash of houseplants dwelled in my bedroom, and their care was squarely in my domain. The ivy was the sole survivor.

I would have liked to nurture something snappier. If a flowering plant could be coaxed to perform without requiring any intervention and with virtually no light, that would have delighted me. But it wasn't going to happen. Heaven knows, I tried to cohabitate with flowering plants, but finally I settled for a steady diet of ivy.

I can't tell you much about the ivy that sat on the desk of my childhood. It was uneventful but alive. The fact that it wandered around looking for light sort of thrilled me. If memory serves, it was straggly. But growth of any sort signified success.

I am so different now. Although anything that rambles around gets the glad hand, it's got to be tight. I am a ruthless pruner, and ivies are periodically pulled into check. Not that ivies are Olympians, but have you noticed that low-maintenance plants get a little extra leeway? Because you are not continually called into their service, they sometimes pull off some capers while your attention is diverted. All of a sudden, I'll notice that the ivies have strayed a little too far. And then a whole lot of snipping goes on.

I most often inflict corrective action in winter, when ivies stretch. During other seasons, growth is more succinct. I generally grow dwarf or medium-size plants, such as *Hedera helix* 'Oak Leaf', *H. helix* 'Needlepoint', and similar tight little numbers. Just like everything else, ivies have come a long way over the years, and there are some mighty cute versions out there. Variegation can also be yours, and the size range runs the gamut. Ditto for growth habit. They all trail, more or less, but you can exercise control according to taste. I cheer on progress, but not the unkempt type.

That's about it for maintenance. It's hard to kill an ivy. If yours has browned tip edges, you were either very negligent or overly generous with water. The container should be neither oversize nor overly cramped. Another cause of leaf drop might be a hot and dry house. Severe lack of humidity can fell anything, and it's probably not great for you or your sinuses, either. Ivies might just be the canaries of the plant kingdom. They don't go down easy. If they die, something is drastically wrong.

I cover my prejudice against hanging baskets in the hoya section. Instead of going that route, you might try a tall container and let your ivy droop down. There is no point in spending too much time or money on an exciting pot because it will probably be lost behind the foliage in short order. I usually grow ivies on a plant stand or table that needs a little softening with leaves. I just let them drape gracefully over the edge to give the sense of carefree abandon, which everyone could use in their home. And nature is the best kind.

I grew *Hedera helix* 'Oak Leaf' in a terrarium on the rocks.

IVY

Hedera helix

EASIEST

SIZE	Drapes down
FOLIAGE	Leaves have various shapes, but a triangularly lobed configuration is the norm
OTHER ATTRIBUTES	A wonderful ground cover below other plants
EXPOSURE	East or west is optimal; north can be tolerated
WATER REQUIREMENTS	Keep soil moderately moist
OPTIMUM NIGHTTIME TEMPERATURE	50–70°F (10–21°C)
RATE OF GROWTH	Medium to fast
SOIL TYPE	Rich, humusy potting soil with compost included
FERTILIZING	Early spring to late autumn
ISSUES	Can be prone to scale; can drop leaves if continually dried out
COMPANIONS	Begonias, ferns, nerve plants, peace lilies, peperomias, philodendrons, and pileas

Whenever Marianne
comes and goes, she
passes a massive
Hedera helix
'Needlepoint' trained
as a topiary in an
urn stationed in the
mudroom.

WANDERLUST

Marianne Vandenburgh doesn't have a lot of extra time for fussy houseplants, which is why she focuses on ivies. Originally the *Hedera Helix* 'Needlepoint' topiary was part of the ambiance in Marianne's immense high Victorian bed-and-breakfast. "I got it as a two-inch plant," she recalls. "It took forever to get going, but it became this happy tree." When she moved to a more compact contemporary house, most of the larger houseplants couldn't make the leap. But the ivies came along, and Marianne is glad: "It's amazing what these things do to your life."

There is a mind-boggling span between the originally adopted cutting and the behemoth that now greets you in the mudroom. Eventually she moved it into a wrought iron urn. Her next act of overindulgence was to give it a pyramid-shaped metal topiary frame, and the ivy was only too happy to respond in kind. "It's almost too much plant to love," Marianne admits. But she wouldn't be without it. Her children and grandchildren live in a different continent, and she notes, "With my family so far away, I have all this mothering pent up." Whenever she walks by the ivy, she pinches it to encourage dense growth. The ivy loves it.

Maybe the ivy likes it too much, because at this point it would require several brawny men to move it. Fortunately, it is fine in a room that plunges down to 45°F (7°C) in the depths of winter, and that's a great solution for ivies that outgrow your heated living space. Meanwhile, smaller ivies lend the contemporary house a sense of warmth and greenery. Each ivy is given a slam-bang presentation fit for a thoroughbred. Other plants get prime positions, but ivies are fine in a spot where nothing else will grow. Plus, they "are okay with being left alone." And that's a relief, because Marianne is a chef-caterer. That's not to say she doesn't appreciate and applaud her houseplants. She is busy, but she always takes time to bask in the glory of her surroundings.

Taking cuttings is a snap (literally) with ivies, so Marianne incorporates them into her so-called natural history museum.

KALANCHOE

You can find panda plants (*Kalanchoe tomentosa*) just about anywhere. Try pairing one with *Kalanchoe beharensis* 'Maltese Cross' in a colander—both are diehards.

Want weird? Have I got freaky for you. Kalanchoes are all oddballs, dressed in outfits you would not believe. Whoever does the wardrobes for sci-fi movies should check them out for inspiration.

Kalanchoes are outlandish, outrageous, otherworldly, and absolutely enthralling succulents. When friends arrive at my house, there's plenty to see. What do they always remark on? The kalanchoes.

And it's not just one kalanchoe that grabs the spotlight. They are all adorned to steal the show. Many have far-out foliage. Devil's backbone (*Kalanchoe daigremontiana*) has swollen leaves speckled like a guinea hen and tiny rosettes lining the edges of each leaf, panda plant (*K. tomentosa*) sports velveteen gray leaves edged in brown like bear paws, Maltese cross (*K. beharensis*) boasts Excalibur-shaped gray felted leaves dusted in cinnamon, and flapjacks (*K. thyrsiflora*) has round paddle-shaped leaves that form a dramatic rosette. That's just a once-over-lightly of the greatest hits. And they are all virtually indomitable. You can hardly kill them

The kalanchoe clan also has you covered when it comes to flowers. Best known is flaming Katy, *Kalanchoe blossfeldiana*, which everyone breaks out for the winter holidays. If you need to give a gift but don't want to saddle the recipient with a full-time job, like a poinsettia or cyclamen, flaming Katy is the present for you. It comes in Christmas red, white, yellow, pink, salmon, and orange. There are double versions that look like a cluster of rosebuds as well as singles that resemble little open-faced starbursts bundled together. And they never stop producing those color-packed clusters throughout the winter season. You can virtually forget them (like if you need to go on vacation) and they will keep on perking along. But if you're home, chances are you'll be giving them plenty of attention because they stage a look-twice sort of presentation. However, don't bother to bring the watering can along when you come to worship at their feet, because they rarely need water or any other form of kibitzing. And flaming Katy is not alone. *Kalanchoe fedtschenkoi* and *K. pumila* have more intriguing foliage than flaming Katy, but their flower power isn't sufficient to put them into the big time, commercially speaking. That's not to say you shouldn't welcome them into your little kingdom. Plus, they follow in the family's low-maintenance footsteps.

It may seem obvious that I'm fond of kalanchoes. Who wouldn't fall for a plant that causes everyone to be jealous and yet requires no upkeep? They all perform best in a sunny south-facing window, but most of mine dwell in east or west and they look equally great. Indeed, my flaming Katy sat beside the kitchen sink last winter because I needed a little spark while doing the dishes. The light source was a west-facing window across the room. Did it pout? Not for a moment. Did it stop blooming? Never. In fact, it was almost appallingly prolific.

I'm a big supporter of succulents in general, and if you add in all of this plant's attributes, wonderful things are bound to happen. Any kalanchoe is a stand-alone star. But consider letting it shine in combination with fellow succulents in a collective planter. Add the felty Maltese cross and panda plant to other matte-surfaced kalanchoes and succulents, or combine the blue leaves of *Kalanchoe pumila* with other

Want weird that you can share? Devil's backbone (*Kalanchoe daigremontiana*) has rosettes lining each leaf that you can remove and pot separately.

hues and the finished product is going to send everyone into orbit. Or try a lineup of flaming Katy in a window box. Very little care and maintenance is needed. That's what makes them great combo players. Even though you are bundling a crowd of plants together, all these individuals require minimal water. Fertilizing is not really necessary with most succulents, including kalanchoes. You can feed them if you want, but they look better grown mean and lean.

There is one chore you might need to incorporate into your routine. Be sure to rotate a combination planter periodically (once every two to three weeks should do the trick) to let all the amassed occupants receive the benefit of the sunbeams. That's the sum total of your physical involvement. Beyond that, be prepared for the barrage of requests from friends who will be begging for rosettes from your devil's backbone. These plantlets send down roots with little or no provocation. They will make you mighty popular.

KALANCHOE
Kalanchoe

ALSO CALLED flaming Katy, panda plant, devil's backbone, Maltese cross

EASIEST

SIZE	Ranging from 6 to 15 inches (15 to 38 cm) high, depending on the variety
FOLIAGE	Succulent, wonderfully bizarre and varied, in a broad color range
OTHER ATTRIBUTES	Some kalanchoes produce beautiful blossoms, particularly flaming Katy
EXPOSURE	South is best; east or west also works
WATER REQUIREMENTS	Can tolerate dry soil
OPTIMUM NIGHTTIME TEMPERATURE	50–70°F (10–21°C)
RATE OF GROWTH	Medium
SOIL TYPE	Sandy potting soil, such as cactus and succulent growing mix
FERTILIZING	Unnecessary; if you feel the urge, early spring to late autumn
ISSUES	Some kalanchoes can stretch with age; simply cut them off at the base and most send up new growth. *Caution! The ASPCA lists kalanchoes among the most toxic plants to pets*
COMPANIONS	Display with fellow succulents (a combination planter is an option); aloes, euphorbias, rhipsalis, and senecios also like similar conditions

MAIDENHAIR VINE

Sometimes you just need something frizzy in your home. Maidenhair vine serves that function.

Enough with the dour-faced aspidistras. Not only is it time to add some levity, but frizzy arms and legs would also be a nice touch. And wouldn't a plant that grows by leaps and bounds be welcome beside a bunch of slow-but-steady reliables? Bring on the clowns. Maidenhair vine certainly qualifies.

You've got to love *Muehlenbeckia complexa* for its sheer energy alone. Although it produces flowers, you are never going to notice them unless you happen to walk around with a magnifier. The fruit is interesting to look at—if you have good eyesight and like itty-bitty odd things. It resembles a translucent version of the little prongs that hold a diamond in its setting. But there is no diamond. Instead, there's a little black crumb at the center. The foliage is roundish and dark green on wiry black stems. These stems are the main story for the maidenhair vine. The plant can go from 3 to 36 inches (7 to 91 cm) in a matter of months.

Watching it gain momentum is just plain fun. If you like big hair, you are going to love muehlenbeckias.

I've seen maidenhair vine used in terrariums. I advise arming yourself with a pair of scissors if you ever open the lid of your little glass jar. Chances are it will jump out like a hybrid between steel wool and my hair (check out my portrait and you'll see what I mean). Maidenhair vine does fine with the high humidity and low light in a terrarium, but it does not need special conditions.

I usually let my maidenhair vine just roam free. Like my outdoor garden, the interiorscape is a combination of architectural plants that form orbs and spikes mingled with plants that have more free-form shapes. The frizzy element loosens up the display and makes me smile. That's a critical role. You need the punctuation marks, and you also need the froth in the middle. That's what makes an indoor garden go round.

Although I let my muehlenbeckia do its thing, many gardeners leash the

MAIDENHAIR VINE
Muehlenbeckia complexa

ALSO CALLED **wire vine**
EASY

SIZE	This rambunctious vine can engulf anything posthaste
FOLIAGE	Tiny, roundish dark green leaves against black shiny stems
OTHER ATTRIBUTES	Often used with topiary structures to form fun shapes quickly
EXPOSURE	South, east, or west
WATER REQUIREMENTS	Keep soil moderately moist; do not allow it to dry out
OPTIMUM NIGHTTIME TEMPERATURE	50–70°F (10–21°C)
RATE OF GROWTH	Very fast
SOIL TYPE	Ideally humusy potting soil with compost included; will grow in almost anything
FERTILIZING	Early spring to late autumn; tolerates forgetful feeding
ISSUES	Keep those shears handy
COMPANIONS	Agaves, aglaonemas, aloes, begonias, bromeliads, hoyas, ivies, kalanchoes, mosses, nerve plants, peperomias, pileas, pothos, prayer plants, rhipsalis, scheffleras, and snow roses

plant's enthusiasm for groping onto any sort of support and put it to work covering topiary forms. You see muehlenbeckia everywhere from florist shops to supermarkets shaped around heart forms, crowns, and geometric shapes. You'll have to intervene to keep any semblance of the shape from turning into a kinky blob. But if you like easy hands-on projects, this is for you.

If you give this easygoing comedian a sunny position, it will grow like a maniac. Station it in indirect light and it will also grow pretty darn rapidly. Slight overwatering is okay, if you tend to err in that direction. Drastic underwatering can be a little more stressful for the vine and might even lead to dieback and leaf drop. I suggest providing sufficient root room to prevent frequent drying out. As for the other elements of cultivation, there is no need to go crazy with the fertilizer. Muehlenbeckia is native to New Zealand and Australia, which says a lot about its tolerance for poor soil. The only high-maintenance task might have to do with shearing. Don't be afraid to vent all your scissorhand tendencies. Although the wiry stems look a little fragile, they will be fine with a stern haircut and will branch out as a result. And a maidenhair vine with a haircut will look a lot like a maidenhair vine that has been left to grow wild and woolly for a few weeks.

MEDINILLA

Although it doesn't look tough as nails, *Medinilla myriantha* is amazingly durable.

Medinilla and I have a pact. As long as I keep pouring on the water, it will continue to pump out the blossoms. Considering it is late November as of this writing, this deal works really well for me. Black Friday looks like it will be just another dark day in a long series of blah weather, so I'll take all the bright color I can get. My medinilla (aka Malaysian grapes) is definitely doing its part.

I originally picked up *Medinilla myriantha* at the supermarket. It is not a particularly common item to find wedged between the birthday balloons and the braided bamboos, but I happened to get lucky. And the fact that it was still alive after a heavy dose of supermarket-inflicted neglect says a lot. Although *M. myriantha* might look far too ritzy to be filed in the indestructible category, it's a trouper. The plant was wilted pathetically when I brought it home, resembling the botanical version of a Humane Society rescue victim, but it snapped out of its deep funk when I gave it a

swank container, beefy soil, and generous water. I shook off a large portion of the original potting soil (if you could call it soil—more like mulch) and downsized the container slightly to fit into my space. Sometimes demotions are necessary when a plant comes into the flock. And it was fine with snugger root accommodations. In fact, it burst into blossom.

The plant has been blossoming ever since, and the package is most impressive. The broad, 6-inch-plus (15 cm) pleated leaves are enough to recommend this to every aspiring houseplant grower. But medinilla combines chic foliage with the equally posh plump clusters of small peach-pink blossoms. The flowers remain in bud stage for quite a while. By the time they fully open, they are usually on the way to falling off, but that's fine. Lots of clusters synchronize simultaneously, followed by nonedible purple berries.

Medinillas tend to steal the show, so give the plant a presentation befitting its star status. Its 36-inch (91 cm) dimensions alone command

The nickname Malaysian grapes refers to the clusters of pink flowers followed by nonedible purple berries.

a lot of attention. I chose a classical container with garlands and a whitewashed finish for mine. You'll need something weighty, as the growth can get hefty and send it into a tailspin without proper ballast. Be prepared for the plant to eventually occupy as much space as a small citrus tree. Although this will take years, you will never part with a medinilla once you've witnessed it in action. Plan ahead. Devoting a window to its grandeur would not be a bad way to proceed.

Medinilla myriantha does not demand a south-facing window, although it does not mind being treated like a sun-worshipper. I give it east or west, and it is fine with both. Fertilizing is not an issue. Considering how poor the soil was upon

MEDINILLA
Medinilla

ALSO CALLED **Malaysian grapes**
EASY

SIZE	Ranging from 24 to 36 inches (61 to 91 cm) high or larger; can become a shrub indoors
FOLIAGE	Broad deep green leaves with pleats
OTHER ATTRIBUTES	Wonderful grape-like clusters of pink flowers throughout autumn and winter, followed by purple nonedible berries
EXPOSURE	South is best; east or west also works
WATER REQUIREMENTS	Very thirsty
OPTIMUM NIGHTTIME TEMPERATURE	60–70°F (15–21°C)
RATE OF GROWTH	Slow
SOIL TYPE	Rich, humusy potting soil with compost included
FERTILIZING	Early spring to late autumn
ISSUES	Drinking habit can be a deal-breaker if you're not home
COMPANIONS	This is a stand-alone specimen, but begonias, nerve plants, orchids, and prayer plants might grow in tandem

arrival, I suspect it can tolerate an unpredictable feeding schedule. If you are feeling generous, give it food every three to four weeks (I use fish emulsion) from March through November, when light levels are spurring on growth. It will be grateful, but will not pout when you forget. However, it is a drinker. Of the many plants in my domain, the medinilla seems to need water nearly daily. If that is a problem, this might not be the botanical buddy for you. But I figure that there are plenty of potential houseplant growers with itchy watering fingers who might be a good match for a thirsty companion. If that sounds like you, go for it. You won't be disappointed.

Not only do they have statuesque
forms that lend themselves to
bonsai, but *Coprosma* 'Rainbow
Surprise' and *C.* 'Tequila Sunrise'
also sport colorful leaves.

MIRROR PLANT

wanted to throw some curveballs into this book rather than just give you a tour of the typical suspects. Many great stoic houseplants are not stocked in supermarkets and big-box stores. That doesn't mean they aren't worthy; they just haven't hit the spotlight yet. I hope mirror plants soon get their well-earned moment in the sun.

I mean that figuratively, because the mirror plant (*Coprosma*) does not demand bright light, and that's one incentive toward adding it to your bucket list. There are many other reasons, but I'll start with the foliage. The leaves are colorful and glossier than your patent leather Mary Janes. In the past few years, I've picked up some real doozies (I mean that in a good way) in my travels. At Landcraft on Long Island, I found *Coprosma* 'Rainbow Surprise' with 1-inch-long (2.5 cm) slender leaves, each with a bright green center surrounded by an irregularly patterned cream, pink, and red edging. It pops from a distance, and it reads like a

kaleidoscope. Then, while visiting Avant Gardens in Massachusetts, *C.* 'Tequila Sunrise' called to me. That one has a mix of dark green, chartreuse, and mahogany on each shiny leaf. Want something a little more toned down? Go for *C. kirkii* 'Variegata', which has tiny, orzo-size green leaves surrounded by cream margins on stems that love to grow horizontally. In no time at all you can train this plant to be an instant espalier.

Beyond the festive foliage, I love the mirror plant's stature. It is like the Japanese maple of the windowsill. Without a whole lot of manicuring it just naturally assumes an articulate stance. The branches become woody from an early age. They start making graceful gestures while still in 4-inch (10 cm) containers. If you want to do a little sculptural work with the plant, you've got a bonsai in a blink. Nobody is going to believe you didn't labor over the clipping and shaping of a coprosma for years when they see the art you've wrought. Any coprosma is a willing target for training.

Beyond working any bonsai inclinations out of my system without all the wiring and obsessing, I use the mirror plant to create a mini habitat. Like false and Ming aralias, coprosma looks like a little tree. Plant a few together and you've got a forest. Not only have you shrunk the woods in which you love to hike, but the scene is perpetually clad in autumn foliage because of the natural coloration on mirror plant leaves.

No matter how cramped I keep the roots or how frequently I forget to water, my coprosma doesn't seem to drop leaves. I keep thinking it's going to mutiny, but the protest never comes. It tends to be thirsty, and ideally you should water it regularly, especially if you keep the roots crammed into a bonsai-ish container. Depending on the cultivar you choose, the branches can become woody with leaves spaced far apart, which looks like the plant is flexing its muscles. If you want to give it a south-facing window, this New Zealand native will love it. But it likes east or west equally well, so feel free to save your prime real estate. Although flowers are not in the cards no matter what sort of accommodations you provide, with those colorful leaves to relish, you've got enough.

MIRROR PLANT
Coprosma
EASIEST

SIZE	Remains 12 to 24 inches (30 to 61 cm) high for quite a while; can eventually grow into a small shrub
FOLIAGE	Small and colorful
OTHER ATTRIBUTES	Can be used to mimic a mini tree
EXPOSURE	South, east, or west
WATER REQUIREMENTS	Keep soil moderately moist
OPTIMUM NIGHTTIME TEMPERATURE	50–65°F (10–18°C)
RATE OF GROWTH	Slow
SOIL TYPE	Rich, humusy potting soil with compost included
FERTILIZING	Early spring to late autumn
PROPAGATION	By cuttings, but woody rooting hormone might be helpful
ISSUES	Can get scale
COMPANIONS	Aralia, ficus, ivies, mosses, nerve plants, pileas, and prayer plants

MOSS

Whether you call them spike moss or club moss, selaginellas lend themselves to combos. Here *Selaginella kraussiana* 'Aurea' is paired with plain old creeping Charlie, *Pilea involucrata*.

Everyone should find a houseplant with which to waltz into the sunset. To achieve that chemistry, I have to factor in all personality types. I fall into the breezy, preoccupied category. I tend to blow my plants a kiss while barreling back and forth through the house and out the door. I also lean toward underwatering. That's fine with most of the plants in this book, but the mosses take offense. If you are an indoor gardener who is wired to pour on the water, mosses are for you.

I am referring to *Selaginella* mosses, often called club mosses or spike mosses. They are relatively easy houseplants compared to the breed of mosses that grow on your walkways and in the forests outdoors. Most woodland mosses are a bear to grow in a home. Don't even go there. Those fussbudgets require a constant pipeline to moisture as well as sauna-like humidity situations. They look adorable, but you don't want moss maintenance as a full-time job. Even in a terrarium they are perpetually

in the intensive care unit.

On the other hand, selaginellas are a snap. They will wilt and eventually perish if you allow them to continually dry out (an infraction or two is generally tolerated, as long as you make amends rapidly). Gardeners who don't want that burden should skip right along to the sempervivums. But I'm sure there are people who would best be matched up with a plant that prefers to be kept moderately moist. Given regular drinks, selaginellas are golden—and infinitely useful.

Selaginellas look sufficiently like woodland mosses to create the sense of a forest dell in your living room. I always keep a few reserves on hand. Since I admit to occasional lapses in my watering schedule, I pair my selaginellas with plants that I dote on. Most often I grow them in tandem rather than giving them stand-alone billing. Need something to cover the soil around a camellia stem or any indoor tree? Want something to jazz up the base of a dracaena, ZZ plant, or any other green thing that shoots up with

bulk above but has chicken legs below? Selaginellas to the rescue. In many cases, the top of a tall plant basks in the light of a window, but the container and its rim are not in the sunbeams. Selaginellas love low light. In separate containers, I grow them with begonias and African violets that share their affinity for indirect illumination. In combo scenes, I tuck them between ferns to spark the memory of nature hikes when I can't get into the woods. If I grow them solo, I pair my spike moss with a container that needs a little bouffant on top, letting their spongy green mats expand over the edges. As Einstein will attest, the plump, verdant cushion of a selaginella is infinitely pettable (although sometimes the moss doesn't fare so well). I am also prone to giving it a little pat.

Selaginellas are also my go-to plants for terrariums. I always have a Mason jar filled with club moss on hand. Sometimes I tuck one into an old-fashioned screw-on lid of a vintage tinted canning jar, set it upside down, and let it

A kick line of tiny pots filled with *Selaginella kraussiana* 'Brownii' on a tool caddy is a mini landscape condensed into less than 36 inches (91 cm) of space.

grow. That jar can entertain for a year or more without requiring replanting, and it makes a great hostess gift.

I veer straight toward *Selaginella kraussiana* 'Aurea' for most of my projects because its fuzzy foliage adds volume with lightning speed and the sparkling chartreuse leaves

complement many plants. You could certainly go with the plain version if deep green is more useful for your projects. In fact, the entire *S. kraussiana* clan is equally amenable for easy growing, including cunning tussock-forming 'Brownii' and 'Variegata', often sold as 'Frosty Fern'. Peacock moss (*S.*

uncinata) is a showstopper with shimmering purple leaves, but it browns easily and never looks tidy. Even if you keep it watered religiously, grooming is continually required. Similarly, red *S. umbrosa* is a challenge and can cause heartbreak. You're welcome to try them, but don't come crying to me when things fail to go your way.

Beyond attention with the watering can, your moss prefers the indirect light of an east- or west-facing window. The beauty of mosses is that they do not need to sit directly in sunbeams. You can stage them below the window level or shadow them with other plants. Mosses are custom crafted for those interminable winter days when the sun is going to shine again tomorrow, or maybe the day after that. In fact, in a south-facing window they might bleach out or burn. If south is all you've got, simply pull them away from the light source. Low indoor temperatures are not generally a problem for *Selaginella kraussiana* because it is hardy to Zone 9. Any home environment temperature that is warm enough for you will be fine with it. Very hot temperatures can cause the bouffant to fizzle, and very low humidity can be an issue. Misting would be a full-time job, so go the practical route of a humidifier instead. Your complexion will thank you for it.

MOSS
Selaginella

ALSO CALLED **club moss and spike moss**
EASY

SIZE	Forms a mounded tuft above the soil surface
FOLIAGE	Lacy green or chartreuse
OTHER ATTRIBUTES	Great for low-light conditions or to form so-called socks beneath other plants
EXPOSURE	East or west; north is also possible
WATER REQUIREMENTS	Thirsty; keep soil moderately moist
OPTIMUM NIGHTTIME TEMPERATURE	55–70°F (12–21°C)
RATE OF GROWTH	Medium
SOIL TYPE	Rich, humusy, peaty potting soil with compost included
FERTILIZING	Early spring to late autumn
ISSUES	Will not forgive constant forgetfulness with the watering can
COMPANIONS	Aglaonemas, begonias, dracaenas, ferns, ficus, ivies, peperomias, philodendrons, pileas, and ZZ plants

NERVE PLANT

Looking particularly swank in a Floraline urn, *Fittonia verschaffeltii* shares a space with prayer plant, *Ctenanthe burle-marxii* 'Amagris' (in the distance).

With pink or white streaks accenting the leaves of the nerve plant, it's easy to it's easy to see the reason for the common name.

ven Einstein has his bad days. Generally he's a good-natured party animal who gives everyone and everything the glad paw, including mice. But he can be a decidedly cranky kitty when his morning beauty rest is interrupted. As mentioned in the carex section, anything that dangles is in peril. Sometimes he takes it out on an unsuspecting carex blade or pennisetum plume. But there are times when the nerve plant attempts to send a stray arm or leg over the edge of its urn and gets a disciplinary, dislocating swat in return. No matter. In a few weeks the fittonia will be sprawling over the edge again, tempting fate.

Whether you call it nerve, mosaic, or snakeskin plant, fittonia always seems to look tidy without any time investment. *Fittonia verschaffeltii* has bronze leaves with ruby veins. Its offshoot, *Fittonia verschaffeltii* var. *argyroneura*, accents its bronze leaves with a network of silver netting. The end result is elegant but also remarkable enough to warrant a second glance. In the world of indestructibles, there are plenty of easily overlooked individuals. You need a few freaks.

Both the white-veined and red-streaked versions send runners romping around. They eventually spill over the side of a container, teasing Einstein to take out his aggressions (if he hasn't already hit the selaginella, which is another unsuspecting target). Regrowth won't happen overnight, but the fittonia always seems to recoup and branch out more thickly as a result. I can also just tuck any stray severed limbs right back into the soil, and chances are they'll take root.

The nerve plant is fine with low light. Even extremely low light does not faze this turn-the-other-cheek plant. However, growth will be tighter and it will generally look more pulled together if afforded an east- or west-facing window. Beyond that, fittonia is a natural for terrariums, where the moist environment is its mother's milk. Keep a nerve plant's soil damp, but not sopping wet. It might revive from a dead wilt once or twice, but don't try this trick too often. For some reason, the red-veined nerve plant seems to tolerate occasional drought more readily than the white-veined version.

Most people grow fittonias as stand-alone plants. They are certainly sufficiently entertaining to impress without further diversions, but why not push the envelope? I've begun pairing nerve plants with upright, moisture-loving plants that might need socks, such as ficus, Norfolk Island pines, ponytail palms, and scheffleras. The nerve plant forms a ruffled collar below its bedfellows while also tumbling down and thumbing its nose at Einstein's fidgety paws. As long as the urn doesn't take a nosedive, the nerve plant usually gets the last laugh. Or, at least, it survives.

NERVE PLANT
Fittonia

ALSO CALLED mosaic plant, rattlesnake plant, silver net plant
EASY

SIZE	Creeps along the soil surface
FOLIAGE	Bronze with white or red veins
OTHER ATTRIBUTES	Makes a good ground cover below other plants; terrarium worthy
EXPOSURE	East, west, or south; might endure north
WATER REQUIREMENTS	Keep soil moderately moist
OPTIMUM NIGHTTIME TEMPERATURE	50–70°F (10–21°C)
RATE OF GROWTH	Medium
SOIL TYPE	Rich, humusy, peaty potting soil with compost included
FERTILIZING	Early spring to late autumn
PROPAGATION	Easily rooted by cuttings; runners will have roots and can be detached
ISSUES	Will wilt, but revives readily; if you forget to water often, it might get aphids
COMPANIONS	Great for underplanting beneath a low-light-loving, tree-like plant such as ficus or Norfolk Island pine. Also good with ponytail palms, prayer plants, scheffleras, and tradescantia; good with begonias in a separate container

NORFOLK ISLAND PINE

Norfolk Island pine (*Araucaria heterophylla*) forms a little green forest and brings the outdoors inside. Here it is coupled with rhipsalis.

'm a sap for anything that remains windowsill-size but looks like someone brought the forest indoors. You are probably right alongside me with this weakness, especially in midwinter. Granted, plenty of evergreens are dwelling outdoors, but there's something particularly endearing about a miniature Christmas tree that stays small enough to become a roommate inside without any fuss. If you agree, Norfolk Island pine is your volunteer for the job.

I did not plan to live with a Norfolk Island pine over the long haul. I initially acquired a few plants for a holiday photo shoot and then failed to ditch them. As a general policy, I keep extras for as long as they continue looking good without undo fuss. This threesome refused to die. Come spring, they were still looking great even though they had not received one iota of attention over the previous five months. To say they got second-rate treatment during the summer would be to seriously gild the lily. They pretty much went through the torture cycle because they were still not part of the permanent collection (it's a tough application process). By the end of summer, when the only evidence that they had endured drought, an occasional knocking over, and a little kicking around was a couple of nearly imperceptible brown needles, I began to reassess our relationship. Suddenly they began to feel like keepers.

I'm not sure if my Norfolk Island pines grew at all during that time. A whole year has come and gone since they wiggled their way into my life, and they have not added another tier of greenery, or even another needle. Thrill-seekers should look elsewhere. But if you just want to adopt a forest into your living room, this plant is the ideal recruit. If you decide your outlook might be immeasurably uplifted if you put together a cluster of live growing conifers—the kind with roots attached—rather than just deck the halls with a bunch of disembodied boughs, veer straight for this little number. Norfolk Island pine has soft, fully strokeable branches of green needles much like a cryptomeria, but is much more pleasant to the touch. The branches jut out in tiers in perfect Christmas tree formation. Larger versions of *Araucaria heterophylla* can even stand in as a tannenbaum substitute in a pinch. The branches probably cannot support your heavier ornaments, but they can certainly suspend paper chains and the like. And there's plenty of room between tiers to display your origami collection to its best advantage.

I picked up my Norfolk Island pines at the supermarket. I wanted to put them into previously acquired bark-covered vessels, so I did not give them a graduation in container size. Since then, they have been absolutely fine with remaining in suspended animation as far as root and head growth are concerned. I water them when I remember (plenty of lapses occur), I have never repotted them, and I give them indirect light from an east-facing window (and

they're not even directly in the indirectly lit space). They are doing great. They would be equally simpatico with west- and south-facing windows, although south requires more consistent pouring of water. And I keep the place on the cool end of the temperature spectrum. Speaking of temperatures, be warned: *Araucaria heterophylla* is native to an island somewhere between Australia and New Zealand, and anything colder than Zone 9 is going to cause its demise. This conifer cannot be recycled outside for most of us after the holiday season is over. But that's okay, because it can dwell indoors happily ever after without surprising you by adding height, girth, or any other sort of shock.

With almost no effort, I have the mini evergreen woods of my fantasies. I cannot imagine life without my Norfolk Island pines. They have become part of the scene. You might also think about realigning your family traditions. This live tree does not even require you to dig a hole.

NORFOLK ISLAND PINE
Araucaria heterophylla
EASIEST

SIZE		Stays between 12 and 24 inches (30 and 61 cm) high for a long time, but will eventually become a small tree; keeping it tightly potted will slow the growth process
FOLIAGE		Dark green needles, just like a mini conifer
OTHER ATTRIBUTES		Can be a stand-in for a Christmas tree
EXPOSURE		East or west
WATER REQUIREMENTS		Water regularly, but it will tolerate drought
OPTIMUM NIGHTTIME TEMPERATURE		50–70°F (10–21°C)
RATE OF GROWTH		Slow
SOIL TYPE		Humusy potting soil with compost included
FERTILIZING		Early spring to late autumn
ISSUES		Needles can turn brown because of excessive drought
COMPANIONS		Aglaonemas, begonias, crotons, dracaenas, ferns, ficus, ivies, mosses, peperomias, and rhipsalis

PEACE LILY

Although it wasn't love at first sight between the peace lily and me, the plant has won me over. When combined with *Ficus pumila* 'Snowflake' in an enamel basin, what's not to like?

You should have read my original scathing review of the peace lily, *Spathiphyllum*. I pretty much roasted the plant, grousing about its salad-like leaves and complaining about its tendency to loiter in doctor's offices, hospital waiting rooms, and other places I would rather not be. But that was before I adopted one. I have done a complete turnaround: I'm now crazy about peace lilies. I can't get enough of their elegant white sail-like flowers. The newer hybrids on the market blossom profusely and tolerate a lot of abuse (except lack of water, but they bounce back when you forget). They have achieved redemption.

Even though I had an attitude, the rest of the world was already converted because peace lilies can endure a lot of abuse while also tolerating low light. I know you've encountered a peace lily sometime in your life. Have you ever gone to the bank? Besides the other green stuff found in that sort of institution, you will usually run into a spathiphyllum or two. Typically, peace lilies are massed together to serve up a valley of greenery that forms a partition between spaces. They perform this task well because of the volume of greenery each one produces. And sure enough, when NASA conducted a study on air-purifying plants, the peace lily received the highest ratings for air-quality control. They are highly efficient for ridding the air of more pollutants—including formaldehyde, benzene, and ammonia—that most plants do. However, spathiphyllums also top the ASPCA's list of toxic plants for pets. Keep this in mind when growing the plant: As mentioned, they do make a whole lot of foliage to tempt your furry companions.

Of course, it's not only about shiny dark green leaves. Even in low light, the new peace lily hybrids pump out the blossoms. I like the dwarf versions best because the flowers-to-foliage ratio is weighted more in the flower direction. The blossoms are really genteel, forming white sails behind a white cone-like spathe. Each flower has its own stance. All together they look like sailboats bouncing on the waves.

But the flowers weren't the only factor that persuaded me to become a spathiphyllum fan. I like the plant's adaptability. When I started playing with the peace lily, I discovered it could look really snappy in all sorts of situations. I dressed it down in a shabby chic enamel container and it looked wonderfully funky. I paired it with a modern ambiance and it was sleek and swank. It even managed to fit in with a rustic and twiggy type of setting, reminding me of its woodland-based Jack-in-the-pulpit kin.

Provide peace lilies with ample root space. The plant dries out (and wilts) frequently because the roots are quenching bulky and thirsty foliage. Avoid just massing them together in the usual blob. You can do better. Play off the snow white flower color and you'll have a lark. Give peace lilies a chance.

PEACE LILY
Spathiphyllum
EASIEST

SIZE	15 to 20 inches (38 to 50 cm) high
FOLIAGE	Dark green initiating from the base
OTHER ATTRIBUTES	Profuse white Jack-in-the-pulpit-like flowers
EXPOSURE	East or west
WATER REQUIREMENTS	Can wilt if you forget to water
OPTIMUM NIGHTTIME TEMPERATURE	55–70°F (12–21°C)
RATE OF GROWTH	Medium
SOIL TYPE	Humusy potting soil with compost included
FERTILIZING	Early spring to late autumn
ISSUES	Can be prone to leaf diseases if stressed by continual wilting. *Caution! The ASPCA lists peace lilies among the most toxic plants to pets*
COMPANIONS	Companions: Aglaonemas, begonias, crotons, dracaenas, ferns, ficus, ivies, mosses, nerve plants, peperomias, and polka dot plants

PEPEROMIA

Peperomias run the gamut of sizes, and one of the tiniest, *Peperomia glabella*, looks adorable in a millstone.

There are a lot of lookalikes in the indestructible category. Not many gardeners would pass the identification test if quizzed on a lineup of dieffenbachias, dracaenas, and aglaonemas. All the long, slender green leaves splattered with cream tend to blend together. That's one reason peperomias are such a relief. Not only are they indomitable, but they also extend the visual antics on your windowsill into a more jazzy and unexpected realm.

Regardless of whether you know it by name, you've probably encountered a peperomia on your way from the bananas to the grapes in the grocery store. Peperomias can be slapped around without showing visible signs of abuse, so florist departments in supermarkets love them. Take that plant with the thick gray velveteen leaves (I'm thinking of *Peperomia incana*) and put it in a metallic container with an attitude. Or grab that benighted plant with the watermelon markings and stick it in a brick carved with a recess. No matter how shlocky a peperomia appears when you first meet, you can elevate it.

I cannot begin to rattle off all the many permutations that peperomia leaves take. The leaves tend to be succulent and bloated, but that's the only common foliar thread. They range from leaves as large as your fist to foliage smaller than your fingernail. Those leaves often sport watermelon-like stripes (*Peperomia argyreia*) on an oval or round surface. But just as often, marbling or various variegation accents oval leaves. Some peperomias make rosettes (*P. caperata*), some could be dead ringers for sedums (*P. nivalis*), and others form mini trees with a decidedly Dr. Seuss charm (*P. ferreyrae*). They trail (*P. rotundifolia*), they drape (*P. scandens*), they fill just about any position that needs some greenery. But all peperomias share the family characteristic of rattail flowers. Don't blame me for the unfortunate comparison; I think the Victorians coined the correlation. But they were right. Peperomia flowers line long, scrawny

stems to form denuded ropes that evoke a certain rodent's tail.

The leaves are intriguing and diverse and the flowers fall in the yawn category, but what I really admire in a peperomia (besides its stoic fortitude) is the fact that it combines well with other kindred spirits. Peperomias are congenial characters. If you tuck a bunch together, nobody is going to push anyone else around. *Peperomia rubella* will jump around and insinuate itself thinly here and there, but it's not pushy. You can snuggle some *P. orba* 'Pixie' beside a slew of *P. caperata* and *P. griseoargentea* in a communal container with a clear conscience. Nobody is going to get bullied. In fact, they will weave together into a wonderful little ecosystem, which is what peperomias do best. I often use 'Pixie' as an underplanting below taller plants. *Peperomia ferreyrae* can be leggy, so I give it a Peter Pan collar of 'Pixie' to form a picture that is everything but buttoned down. Woodsy or jazzy—peperomias can do both.

I always keep a few *Peperomia clusiifolia* in windowsills that receive inadequate light to nurture greedier houseplants. They have thick, chubby leaves with substance and make a substantial silhouette. Their thick branches interweave in a sinuous way that's sort of sexy. When Einstein sends them

Some peperomias trail, while others stand upright or look like mini trees, like the odd fellows in this chorus line of (left to right) *Peperomia orba* 'Pixie', *P. ferreyrae*, and a wooden shoebox mixed with various peps.

The array of textures available in peperomias creates a habitat in a wooden shoebox, including *Peperomia caperata*, *P. orba* 'Pixie', *P. griseoargentea*, and *P. ferreyrae*.

into the occasional tailspin, they get themselves up and carry on—with maybe a few less leaves. That's when they get dusted off.

As far as cultivation goes, peperomias are incredibly forgiving, and this personality trait has earned them the urban nickname of radiator plant. They did not win the epithet on the basis of any ability to send off heat, but you could conceivably set a peperomia on a radiator without causing its instant death. I wouldn't do that, but they can endure some mighty dry atmospheres. Most will also forgive if you forget to water occasionally, even though they tend to be thirsty plants. *Peperomia ferreyrae* does not suffer in silence, however. If you repeatedly neglect to quench its thirsty puffy leaves, it sheds them. I find the denuded look to be rather handsome, in an offbeat sort of way. But I'm easily entertained.

PEPEROMIA

Peperomia

ALSO CALLED radiator plant

EASIEST

Everyone knows watermelon peperomia, *Peperomia argyreia*, and you can buy it anywhere plants are sold.

SIZE	Some creep over the ground; others form colonies of 4- to 6-inch-high (10 to 15 cm) branches; others stand 12 to 18 inches (30 to 45 cm) tall
FOLIAGE	Usually succulent; extremely varied in form with diverse and handsome streaks, stripes, and variegation
OTHER ATTRIBUTES	Can be planted in unison with other peperomias or similar plants in the same container
EXPOSURE	East or west
WATER REQUIREMENTS	Keep soil moderately moist; most can tolerate occasional lapses in watering
OPTIMUM NIGHTTIME TEMPERATURE	50–70°F (10–21°C)
RATE OF GROWTH	Slow to medium
SOIL TYPE	Rich, humusy potting soil with compost included
FERTILIZING	Early spring to late autumn
ISSUES	Drought can cause some to lose leaves
COMPANIONS	Aglaonemas, aspidistras, begonias, bromeliads, ferns, ficus, hoyas, ivies, and scheffleras

THE PEP TALK

David Whitman and Peter Stiglin display all manner of nature-boy behavior. When weather allows (as well as when it is not so conducive), you'll find these guys wandering in the woods. Not only does nature make their eyebrows shoot up, it also lends character to their shop, Pergola, in New Preston, Connecticut. Being outdoors provides therapy for their busy lives as well. "When I'm in the wilderness," David notes, "I'm most blissful." And it doesn't take much to send him into euphoria: "The simple act of searching the woods forces me to look closely." Pergola is dedicated to sharing that sense of wonder.

Given their druthers, both David and Peter would probably slip into the wild blue yonder permanently, but those would be lean times. That's why they need to bring some of it home to keep them company. "A peperomia on the kitchen table with a bowl of fruit is all any of us really needs," David points out. "You prop up a plant's stems with magnolia branches, for example. How wonderful is that? The plant is just sort of telling you what to do." Rather than continually talking to your plants, listen sometimes.

David and Peter have found themselves leaning toward peperomias because the genus has "so much textural interplay," as David puts it. "Same theme, different avenues. And they all need the same growing conditions." Meanwhile, peperomias find their way into their shop, tucked into everything from odd pieces of driftwood to elegant, sleek hand-thrown terra-cotta. In such settings, peperomias deliver the forest ambiance into the human domain. As Peter and David have found, near proximity to nature can change

Peter and David's homage to peperomias includes *Peperomia nivalis*, *P. caperata* 'Ripple', and *P. orba* 'Pixie'.

your life. "It's the difference between a person in a crowd and a friend. If I have a dialogue with nature, I'll know it better, especially if we bring it into the most intimate environment—our home."

PHILODENDRON

I never thought I'd fall in love with a philodendron. It's not that I had an attitude; the plant just didn't strike me as cohabitation material. I draw the line at scruffy when I invite plants into my home. A dress code isn't necessary, and I'm totally willing to do rehab. But I don't need one more mess in my life.

I was in for a pleasant surprise when I revisited philodendrons. In fact, *Philodendron corda tum* 'Brasil' was among the plants that inspired me to write this book. This plant doesn't break the sound barriers for brave new philodendrons. It isn't drastically different from any old *P. hederaceum* you will find hanging around, except for the bright gold streak running through the deep green leaf. Like all heart-leaved philodendrons, it sends out long, trailing branches that can look creepy if you don't keep them groomed. Because the plants are blasé about any sort of abuse, gardeners tend to dole out a north-facing window and let the free-for-all begin. The end result

doesn't do any philodendron justice. However, you can improve on that image. Wind the foliage around neatly on itself, like you do with your scarf, and you are headed in the right direction. But an east- or west-facing window will make all the difference in keeping the presentation tight rather than straggly. Another little trick I do with 'Brasil' and its kin is to tuck it in with another plant—zonal geraniums are a favorite— like a bow on a Christmas wreath to add an accent. Or I pair it with something retro chic.

Back in my hippie days, I ran into my fair share of fiddle-leaf philodendrons (*Philodendron bipennifolium*), split-leaf philodendrons (*P. bipinnatifidum*), and other large-leaved trailing versions climbing up redwood bark stakes. They didn't stir me even slightly, and they still don't. But they are definitely the plant version of The Big Easy. If you want a large leaf that almost looks like plastic, go for it. And there are new spins on this group that even I could learn to love, such as

'Xanadu', which has deeply cut leaves about the size of your hand.

My current favorites are the versions that have thick, glossy leaves in rust, burgundy, orange, and yellow, like *Philodendron* 'McColley's Finale' and *P.* 'Prince of Orange'. They send off immense leaves from a central base, and they are neat as a pin. They are a great decorating secret for offsetting red furniture or bringing a glowing ember of yellow into a room. They don't really do stunts; in fact, 'McColley's Finale' has not grown perceptively over the past six months. But I'm okay with that.

For a space where nothing else will grow, enlist a philodendron and give the plant a thoughtful presentation. It might just surprise you and gather compliments. What it won't do is hogart your time. All a philodendron needs is a dash of water once a week. You might consider dusting it once in a while, but that's optional. If you do tickle it with the feather duster, be sure to don a 1950s hostess apron. Why garden indoors if you can't have fun?

When this chair was in its glory, snappy *Philodendron cordatum* 'Brasil' had not yet been introduced. Now I can do them both justice.

PHILODENDRON
Philodendron
EASIEST

SIZE	Drapes down vigorously and rapidly; some grow upright standing 18 to 24 inches (45 to 61 cm) high
FOLIAGE	Heart-shaped leaves are the norm; long paddle-like versions are becoming popular
OTHER ATTRIBUTES	Variegated trailers are great for an accent with other plants
EXPOSURE	East or west is optimal; north can be tolerated
WATER REQUIREMENTS	Keep the soil moderately moist; will forgive transgressions
OPTIMUM NIGHTTIME TEMPERATURE	50–70°F (10–21°C)
RATE OF GROWTH	Fast
SOIL TYPE	Rich, humusy potting soil with compost included
FERTILIZING	Early spring to late autumn
ISSUES	Can become unkempt if not groomed and wound neatly
COMPANIONS	Aspidistras, begonias, ferns, ivies, nerve plants, peace lilies, peperomias, pileas, and pothos

PILEA

Aluminum plants, *Pilea cadierei*, look great even when small. But remember that plants in tiny pots need vigilance to make sure they don't dry out.

Every family has its difficult members. Sit down to any Thanksgiving dinner, and you will find that some relatives are smooth while others are prickly. The same is true for plants. Take pileas, for example. You couldn't sabotage *Pilea glauca* if you tried. On the other hand, it's nearly impossible to keep cat's tongue plants, *P. mollis* 'Moon Valley', alive.

Let's focus on the hang-loose pilea contingent, which has several members. Where would I be without *Pilea glauca*? Sometimes it's labeled 'Aquamarine', and it also goes under the term "silver sprinkles." It's a mass of minute leaves each about the size of a child's pinky fingernail covering mahogany-colored trailing stems. Each leaf is shiny and icicle silver with a bluish tinge. It covers the ground like a carpet with a haste that's hard to match. If you turn your head for a couple of weeks, you will find it has walked several inches. It sometimes blossoms, but you're apt to overlook this event because the blooms are almost imperceptible (but they are cute in an overly modest sort of way). I plant it in containers—especially metal, because it matches—and let it meander to evoke a sense of carefree abandon. Even more frequently I pair it with something that has silver speckles in its leaves and let it swarm around the plant's ankles. *Pilea glauca* tolerates low light, but it will get a little bit looser and woolly in those conditions. In slightly brighter light it forms a dense mat.

Pilea depressa does the exact same job, but it's green. The leaves are a smidge larger and it looks like someone stitched the end of the edges, which is an endearing quality if you're prone to examining things up close. It is just as low maintenance as *P. glauca*, and you can enlist it for the same tasks.

I should link up with aluminum plants, *Pilea cadierei*, more often. They are complaisant and colorful, with smallish shiny green leaves marked with mirror-like silver insets. The plant remains under 12 inches (30 cm) for

Pilea glauca 'Aquamarine' covers the ground in no time. This is a gutter section converted into a container (and drilled with some holes), but the pilea camouflages the entire surface.

quite a while, and then it can stretch to twice that size while the leaves gain length. I've never encountered any issues with its care, and it has deep roots in houseplant traditions. Chances are your grandmother grew it.

Pilea peperomioides also belongs to the laid-back branch of the family, but it's not so easy to find on the market. It has perfectly round, shiny leaves that look like little umbrellas with the leaf stem fairly close to the edge. It's never given me any angst, except for the exasperation inherent in trying to hunt up a source. Artillery plants, *P. microphylla*, manage to ricochet their minute leaf segments around and pop up everywhere in other containers. They are equally easy, but be prepared for some weeding chores. Of all the peperomias, it likes the most moisture.

I wish creeping Charlie, *Pilea involucrata*, was more amenable, but it tends to get mildew and other leaf issues. Although it comes in many guises, including silver and bronze forms, I've sent them all to the compost pile over the years. Same for *P. grandis*, which looks lovely for a while and then gives me problems. And don't even think of growing the cat's tongue plant, *P. mollis* 'Moon Valley'. It's absolutely fascinating, with heavily textured leaves that resemble its moniker, yet it never survives

PILEA
Pilea

ALSO CALLED **aquamarine, aluminum plant**
EASIEST

SIZE	Some creep over the ground; others stand 12 to 18 inches (30 to 45 cm) high
FOLIAGE	My favorites are the creeping types with tiny leaves, but upright versions have aluminum-like markings on their foliage
OTHER ATTRIBUTES	Use these as a ground cover below other plants (have fun matching the foliar markings)
EXPOSURE	East or west
WATER REQUIREMENTS	Keep soil moderately moist; most can tolerate occasional lapses in watering
OPTIMUM NIGHTTIME TEMPERATURE	50–70°F (10–21°C)
RATE OF GROWTH	Fast
SOIL TYPE	Rich, humusy potting soil with compost included
FERTILIZING	Early spring to late autumn
ISSUES	Follow the suggestions for pileas that are easy; some can be bears
COMPANIONS	Aglaonemas, aspidistras, begonias, bromeliads, ferns, ficus, hoyas, ivies, nerve plants, peperomias, and scheffleras; use as ground covers below single-stemmed plants

in my house. I categorize it as a greenhouse specimen only. But you can't expect an entire clan to be at your beck and call for home duty. Work with the pileas that are congenial, and enjoy their many gifts.

PLECTRANTHUS

Plectranthus oertendahlii 'Uvongo' is an incredibly versatile plant. In summer it can be part of a mixed container. If you bring it in during winter, you'll have an indestructible houseplant.

I know you've been in this situation. It's autumn and your window box is lush and lovely. It has worked itself into a boast-worthy froth. But frost is predicted. In fact, if you believe the weather forecast, the witching hour for that container will strike later that night. Do you pitch the whole concoction right when it's finally reached wonderful? Of course not. You salvage it.

That was me recently, looking frost in the face with a box filled with plump *Plectranthus oertendahlii* that I'd been fattening all summer. The plectranthus probably cost a princely $5 when I purchased it in early summer for my front porch window boxes—pin money in the greater context of what I spend to spruce up my garden annually. By the time autumn arrived, the plant looked gorgeous. Thanks to some strategic pinching, it had expanded into a portly mound. So I bought the plectranthus a $25 container (are you keeping tabs on the bottom line?), pulled it out of the window box, potted it

individually, and voilà: I had the makings of a slam-bang display that gave me infinite pleasure throughout the winter. The expense for the project multiplied more than threefold. But a bouquet would cost more, and this little achievement lasted much longer than any flower arrangement could.

What really sealed the deal was that the plectranthus was totally hands off. Just as the plant was virtually carefree outdoors, except for occasional watering, it was equally independent inside. The same is true for most of its kin. Plectranthus are close cousins to coleus but even easier, and they are equally simple to propagate. Like coleus, they can get a little stretchy during winter in low light, which is what it was dealing with in front of my French doors. But a few whacks with the pruning shears take care of that. As soon as spring arrives, your plectranthus will be in a position to grow out and refill your window box without further underwriting. You may have splurged on its winter container, but the investment went to a good cause.

And the summer show is just a prelude to what happens in winter. *Plectranthus oertendahlii* has plush leaves netted with silver on the upper surface (there's a stunning version on the market called 'Uvongo' with fully silver leaves) contrasted by burgundy below. The flowers are white and small, but they form a constant candelabra above the plant, and there is hardly a moment in autumn or winter when *P. oertendahlii* pauses from pumping out those flowers. If you forget to deadhead the spent blossoms, the seeds fall into adjacent plants (in my case, there are plenty of ready recipients nearby). Since they spill over the edge of the container, it makes for continuity. My self-sown plectranthus seedlings made the indoor display into the garden that I strive to create, flower echoes and all.

Plectranthus oertendahlii is just one example of what plectranthus can do. Virtually every specimen I've encountered has handsome leaves. Most are thick and more or less felted, and they look like the sort of foliage at which you can (figuratively) throw darts without fear that they'll deflate. Those leaves range in size from 1 inch (2.5 cm) or less to 3 inches (7 cm), they frequently feature notched edges, and they are often heavily textured. Sometimes flowers are in the cards. Plus, there are lots of spins on the Swedish ivy clan (*P. verticillatus* has shiny leaves, while *P. forsteri* is a more velveteen version) that have marbling and variegation on the leaves, although insignificant flowers. But even more prevalent on the market (omnipresent, in fact) is *P.* 'Mona Lavender', which has deep purple velvet leaves. Waving above the foliage is a pageant of 1-inch-long (2.5 cm) tubular mauve blossoms on tall spikes. The plant resembles a lobelia indoors.

One reason I work with plectranthus both indoors

and out is that I love the plant's independent spirit. When I have one foot out the door, the last thing I have to check is the plectranthus. Unless I have forgotten it repeatedly, it will be just fine for a day or two while I'm away. Only constant insults will cause retaliatory action. These plants rarely wilt, and if it comes to that, they generally bounce back. But it is better to treat them humanely to achieve a robust plant. The best of all worlds for a plectranthus would be an east- or west-facing window (south is also fine). Water when the soil is dry, but try not to overwater, especially in winter. Fertilize once a month during the growing season. Keep them deadheaded and be vigilant with the pruning shears, and they'll be fine. With a little planning, you might never have to spend another $5 on a window box plant—you can just bring your plectranthus back outdoors and take cuttings.

PLECTRANTHUS
Plectranthus

ALSO CALLED **Mexican mint**
EASIEST

SIZE	Ranging from 8 to 20 inches (20 to 50 cm) high
FOLIAGE	Often felted and thick with beautiful markings
OTHER ATTRIBUTES	Great for using in carefree window boxes in summer
EXPOSURE	South, east, or west
WATER REQUIREMENTS	Keep soil moderately moist; forgives some forgetfulness
OPTIMUM NIGHTTIME TEMPERATURE	50–70°F (10–21°C)
RATE OF GROWTH	Fast
SOIL TYPE	Rich, humusy, peaty potting soil with compost included
FERTILIZING	Early spring to late autumn
PROPAGATION	Easily rooted by cuttings
ISSUES	Overwatering can cause rot
COMPANIONS	Can be an underplanting in the same pot as medinilla or a prayer plant; couple with begonias, bromeliads, ficus, geraniums, ivies, slipper orchids, snow rose, spider plants, and tradescantia

THE AMATEUR'S GUIDE TO HAIRCUTTING

Great plectranthus aren't just born, they're shaped. The same is true for many of the plants in this book, including alternantheras, begonias, evolvulus, ficus, iresine, peperomias, and snow roses. I never understood why people get all panicky and sweaty when you put a pair of pruners in their hands. Yes, we've all walked out of a salon with a horrid haircut, but this isn't nearly as painful. When you give a plant a trim, you almost always improve its general appearance. And even if you botch it up, it (usually) grows out eventually.

One of the main problems people have with pruning is that it should be done when a plant is in its prime, and nobody wants to cut a great performance short. But think of it as an investment in the future. It is better not to let the plant become straggly before you apply the scissors.

In most cases, the best time to prune is spring and summer, when the plant is poised to make tight new growth. Of course, if a plant is sending up leggy shoots in winter, curtail its urge to stretch and cut it back. But in spring and summer, you're most likely to make cuts that will positively impact the plant's future stature. Think about your goal. If you want the plant to make horizontal growth, clip close to the base of the plant and let side branches expand outward. If you want the plant to make a vase-shaped form, cut slightly further up the stem and continue to snip shoots so the volume above is increased.

When you prune back a branch, be sure to cut immediately above the juncture where new leaves are connected to the stem. That's where side branches are going to sprout. On the other hand, not all leaf junctures have the potential for making new growth, such as with begonias and geraniums. Check the juncture for emerging side growth before you snip. And when you do prune, try to balance your cuts so new growth becomes evenly distributed.

It is very fulfilling to create a supermodel. Once you've begun working to shape a beautiful botanical specimen, it becomes addictive. You'll be taking swipes right and left, and the end result will be brilliant. Think of it as a collaboration. To achieve its full potential, the plant needs a little help from a friend.

POLKA DOT PLANT

Polka dot plants (*Hypoestes phyllostachya*) just beg to be combined with another pattern. I coupled this one with *Ficus pumila* 'Snowflake' in a window box to add a little punch.

ometimes I just want to wing out. You know the feeling. You've been wearing a drab A-line skirt and plain jacket over a button-down Oxford shirt all week, and it's time to let your hair down and jump into your twirly patterned dress. Well, the same is true for houseplants. Aspidistras and peace lilies are all well and good, but occasionally you need a little polka dot plant in your life. *Hypoestes phyllostachya* allows you to go to your happy place without expending a whole lot of effort.

It goes by the names polka dot plant, freckle face, or measles plant, and looks like someone went crazy with the sprinkles while flying over a deep green–leaved plant. There's a magenta-dotted version and a white-dotted edition, and what was once a gangly guy is now more compact. You get a bite-size dose of pizzazz in a small package. The leaves provide the main thrill, and they are sufficiently colorful to fulfill any need for perks. The blossoms are insignificant, but that's okay—flouncing flowers would only detract from the peppered foliage.

Polka dot plants have always been foolproof. The plant is indestructible because it fits almost anywhere you want to tuck a spark of color, and it adapts itself to any growing conditions. Polka dots never monopolize much room, and in that modest footprint they make a cheerful statement. If you need a little splash, no matter if you have sun or shade, the polka dot plant can do the job—although a well-lit east- or west-facing window is preferable. Keep the plant amply watered without allowing it to wilt. It will endure a few transgressions, but continual stress might lead to aphids or mealybugs. If you treat it right, it will perform. Most polka dots on the market are self-branching, which frees you from having to pinch them. But fear not: The versions currently on the market stand less than 6 inches (15 cm) high, so they are not going to become gawky even if you aren't cool with cutting.

In addition to using polka dots as terrarium mainstays, I generally tuck them around a taller plant to serve as a collar of color. But they can certainly serve as stand-alone plants. If you need a lift, pick up several (they often hang out at grocery stores), pot them together in a small planter (you generally need a few to make a statement), and put the display in your kitchen, pantry, or powder room. Or how about giving them as favors at a children's birthday party? Not that they're just for kids—everyone needs to smile.

POLKA DOT PLANT
Hypoestes phyllostachya

ALSO CALLED freckle face, measles plant
EASY

SIZE	Usually less than 6 inches (15 cm) high
FOLIAGE	Maroon with white or red freckles
OTHER ATTRIBUTES	Makes a good ground cover below other plants
EXPOSURE	South, east, or west
WATER REQUIREMENTS	Keep soil moderately moist
OPTIMUM NIGHTTIME TEMPERATURE	50–70°F (10–21°C)
RATE OF GROWTH	Fast
SOIL TYPE	Rich, humusy, peaty potting soil with compost included
FERTILIZING	Early spring to late autumn
PROPAGATION	Cuttings
ISSUES	Can be prone to aphids if you forget to water frequently
COMPANIONS	Great for underplanting beneath a low-light-loving, tree-like plant such as upright ficus, Norfolk Island pines, and scheffleras, or you can grow it with creeping fig, nerve plants, peace lilies, and ponytail palms

PONYTAIL PALM

Working on this book is like having a reunion. It has given me a good excuse to reunite with plants I tended at Logee's Greenhouses many years ago. When I came to Logee's in the 1970s as the first nonfamily member on permanent staff, most of the mature plants in the catacomb of greenhouses earned their keep as stock plants. But a few display plants in the more geriatric greenhouses were relics from several generations back, when the glass houses were more about Victorian indulgence—in anything-green and less about making cold cash.

Originally the greenhouse was the playground of a shoemaker with a penchant for plants but without next of kin. When he passed away in 1892, the greenhouse went to his neighbors, the Logee family. I doubt the ponytail palm that gave the original greenhouses their tropical mood was part of his collection—the hothouse froze during its initial winter with the Logee family and only a jasmine survived. But it was quite possible that Grandpa Logee harbored that particular ponytail palm in his front parlor. The parlor, a testimony to all things high Victorian and horticultural, hadn't changed much with time. But the bulk of its plants, except a few begonias, eventually migrated over to the greenhouses' catchall areas. The fern house was where the ponytail palm dwelled, along with some bona fide palms and other botanical white elephants.

By the time I made the ponytail palm's acquaintance, the plant was no longer in its prime. It had an immense, bloated base that made clear how the plant earned the nickname elephant foot tree. But the foliage end of the display was shaggy. I could see why it was called ponytail palm, but it didn't hold a candle to the breathtaking examples with gently wavy hairdos that I later encountered elsewhere.

But that original ponytail palm, currently called *Nolina recurvata* but known until recently as *Beaucarnea recurvata*, possessed one trait that secured its place in the parlor and later in the Logee collection. Even though it could not be propagated for sale and definitely wasn't pulling its weight in the earnings-per-square-footage arena, the plant required almost no care. There it sat, with its bulging base tapering to a long woody neck and then sending a shower of long leaves flowing out like a fountain. It needed water only twice a week at most. Even in the driest, hottest weather it never cried out for care.

My prototypical ponytail palm introduction was with a plant that had long since burst out of its container. That was my first lesson: Give this plant an ample (but not overly big), shallow, and wide container from the get-go because it is going to expand, and that's a good thing. But although it was sitting in a cracked pot that leaked water like a sieve, the ponytail palm wasn't bothered. And, furthermore, it demanded no direct light. It was perfectly happy in the shade; in fact, it preferred wallowing in the shadows. Ponytail palms can tolerate bright (but not too bright) light, but only if they've been acclimated. Suddenly treating a ponytail to a major dose of lumens will lead to brown leaves.

I pulled out my battered 1890 edition of *Henderson's Handbook of Plants* and found the ponytail palm listed in its pages. I think the word used as a descriptor was *grotesque*, which is pretty much on target—no disrespect intended. The seedlings begin to develop their woody, onion-like, aboveground bulbs fairly early in the game, and those water-retaining units continue to swell with time. In nurseries, baby ponytail palms are generally sold as little clusters. The sooner you divide off individual ponytails, the faster they'll reach the mature fountain effect—if you don't overwater, which can be a killer. If you keep in mind that ponytails were designed to store water in their swollen parts in preparation for drought, you'll be on safe ground.

Ponytail palms can be purchased as small plants and usually have several bulbs together. You can leave them in tandem until they begin to swell.

Henderson's Handbook mentions ponytail palm's flowers. The plant is in the lily family, but I have never witnessed the blossom show in person. Apparently it looks like a plume of white or a gigantic polygonum (aka knotweed or fleece vine). *Henderson's* refers to 4,000 to 5,000 tiny flowers clustered together on an eruption that juts up 36 inches (91 cm) or more. This could be a handful if it occurred indoors, but that's unlikely to happen. More of an issue is what to do when the foliar display becomes too tall and needs to be disciplined, which is the issue I most often have to field when I'm taking calls on the radio. You can cut the ponytail back and it will sprout several ponytails from the wound. It won't have the same shock value, but it will look okay.

If you like grotesque—and I must admit I find it immensely appealing—you should celebrate it. Rather than treating the plant like a slightly dorky relic, harness

PONYTAIL PALM
Nolina recurvata

ALSO CALLED **elephant foot tree**
EASIEST

SIZE	Eventually 24 to 36 inches (61 to 91 cm) or taller
FOLIAGE	Long, thin, grass-like, gently curving leaves flow like a fountain
OTHER ATTRIBUTES	Forms a large bloated bulb at the base
EXPOSURE	East or west; sudden bright light will cause scorching
WATER REQUIREMENTS	Thanks to the water-retaining bulb it can endure periods without water, but don't overdo it
OPTIMUM NIGHTTIME TEMPERATURE	55–70°F (12–21°C)
RATE OF GROWTH	Slow
SOIL TYPE	Humusy potting soil with compost included
FERTILIZING	Early spring to late autumn
ISSUES	Can become stretchy over time—that's when surgery is necessary
COMPANIONS	Aglaonemas, begonias, crotons, dracaenas, ferns, ficus, ivies, mosses, nerve plants, peperomias, and polka dot plants

that oddity. This sleeper has the potential to steal the scene. Play up its Victorian roots and pot it in an urn, perhaps something wrought iron and gargoyled. Inside you'll have the fountain of your dreams without the splash. Or try a matched pair of containers. You'll suddenly turn a throwaway moment into a heart-stopper.

Ponytail palms require very little care. You might need to clip the ends of the leaves if they turn brown, but cutting off too much will ruin the coiffure. If the bottom leaves turn yellow, pull them from the base. The only thing you really need to worry about is yellowing leaves. That's what I love about plants that have been grown for centuries: The fact that they lived in our homes when the environment wasn't easy says everything about their personalities.

POTHOS

Silver satin, *Scindapsus pictus* 'Argyraeus', is a pothos of a whole different color. It's absolutely elegant, especially in a verdigris umbrella stand.

Some plants are used as spaceholders in offices and waiting rooms. Like elevator music, they are just supposed to lighten the mood. A plant that has a tendency to die or look like it is headed in that direction would not qualify for this job. Pothos, on the other hand, is an ideal applicant.

I never wanted my home to look like a doctor's office. When I walk in after a road trip, I don't want to see something I associate with a strep infection. So *Epipremnum aureum* 'Marble Queen' was not on my must-have list. Neither were any of the chartreuse or other white- and yellow-streaked variations of the typical pothos. I understand why the plant has endeared itself to doctors, as it is virtually unkillable (the medical profession likes that sort of thing). But for the intimacy of my home? Maybe not.

For anyone drawing a blank when trying to picture a typical pothos, here are a few hints. It has long, trailing stems clad with fist-size oval leaves that are almost heart shaped. Think of a philodendron and you're nearly there. The foliage is waxy and pale green, and it generally has irregular yellow marbling or streaking. You probably bumped into it at the bank today—you just don't remember the encounter.

I didn't have a policy against pothos; I just wasn't inspired. Then I met silver satin and the alarms went off. *Scindapsus pictus* 'Argyraeus' is a whole different animal, with matte forest green leaves that are shaped like a trowel blade. They curve slightly and irregularly on the stem, like a slew of parentheses. Each leaf has matte alligator-like silver markings. Mine joined the fold about six months ago as a cluster of stems tucked into a container. Since then the stems have swooped down to form graceful arcs. They're not breaking any speed records, but the plant is very swank.

Perhaps you've noticed I am not a major advocate for hanging baskets. When you are growing indoors, caring for a plant that is dangling aloft is a cumbersome chore fraught with the possibility of causing drips and other catastrophes. I hate to imagine the fate of a hanging plant with dangling leaves swaying above Einstein. My Plan B is a tall cylinder made of metal with a verdigris finish. It was probably meant to be an umbrella stand, but after a few well-aimed drainage holes were drilled into the bottom, it got a whole new gig. You could also recruit a pedestal urn for the purpose. Anything that elevates the plant to let its stems swoop down is going to work.

Pothos can be riveting, so do your part to give it a toothsome role. While you're at it, place the plant where it might get noticed. The beauty of all pothos, including silver satin, is that they can dwell where light levels are low. That means you can push a container into the center of a room without suffering ill consequences. Not many plants are so obliging. And because it dangles, you can pair pothos with other upright plants, such as Chinese evergreen (*Aglaonema*) or aspidistra. You can set up something quite glam without cluttering a window or your office.

People boast about how long their pothos vines are trailing. But is a Rapunzel-like plant really the goal? A long, thin stem with sparse leaves can be an extended eyesore if it's straggling 40 feet (12 m). I prefer a dense nest of leaves at the base with a few articulate stems showering down. You can snip your pothos and easily root the cuttings, just like a philodendron. The easiest method would be to stick those stems back into the soil and keep it lightly moist.

Given how fond I am of silver satin, you would think it would get all sorts of TLC. Wrong. It has gone through the stress testing cycle, and it succeeded gloriously. Aside from a few brown leaves, the plant lived on unscathed when I forgot to water. Despite the fact that it dwells dangerously close to a heat vent, it is just fine. And the typical pothos are even harder to hurt. I like that in a houseplant.

POTHOS
Scindapsus pictus and *Epipremnum aureum*

EASIEST

SIZE	Drapes down
FOLIAGE	Rounded to heart-shaped leaves; the waxy version with cream or white markings is the norm, but a gray edition is much more handsome
OTHER ATTRIBUTES	If done right, can be absolutely swank
EXPOSURE	East or west is optimal; north can be tolerated
WATER REQUIREMENTS	Best to keep the soil moderately moist; will forgive transgressions
OPTIMUM NIGHTTIME TEMPERATURE	50–70°F (10–21°C)
RATE OF GROWTH	Medium to fast
SOIL TYPE	Rich, humusy potting soil with compost included
FERTILIZING	Early spring to late autumn
ISSUES	Can become unkempt if not groomed and wound neatly. *Caution! The ASPCA lists pothos among the most toxic plants to pets*
COMPANIONS	Begonias, ferns, ivies, nerve plants, peace lilies, peperomias, philodendrons, and pileas

PRAYER PLANT

Ctenanthe burle-marxii 'Amagris' (in the foreground) and *Ctenanthe lubbersiana* 'Brazilian Snow' are pulled to the side of my bathroom window to allow the beams to fall on plants (such as the rhizomatous begonia) that need more light.

Although hybridizers jazzed up many indestructibles only recently, prayer plants were always dressed to impress. You could easily design a room around their markings. A prayer plant can offset the main elements of any decor. Move over, faux zebra-striped rug and ikat-slipcovered sofa; you've got competition. If you have a more traditional environment, a ctenanthe can be the sole spark of pizzazz.

The interior accessory analogy is a good one, considering that prayer plants run the gamut in their design range. Without any human intervention they tend to be tricked out in lots of bizarre color combinations, with red streaks emblazoning spotted and splashed leaves and that sort of big bang. Their leaf colors can be lush shades of browns and fawn mixtures, or they can be ruby red streaked with greens and cream. Even the most sedate prayer plants have plenty to arrest your eye, but most tend toward bolder combinations that read like tie-dye.

That's why pairing them with daring decor feels so apropos. But then again, put a prayer plant in a domain with earth tones and it will look like the carnival in the corner. You could skip the token vase of tulips and display a permanent exhibit of prayer plants instead.

The dimensions of prayer plants are another boasting point and design benefit. Their size span is refreshing. Most groups of plants keep within a limited size range, but members of the Marantaceae range from individuals with tiny, thumbnail-size leaves to gigantic plants with foliage that stretches more than 12 inches (30 cm) in length. Some form a neat little nest on the ground, while others reach 36 inches (91 cm) in height. This is the sort of interior accessory that reads from across the room.

I debated whether to include prayer plants in this book. If you took a survey and polled all the members of this clan, you would probably come up with a scoreboard stacked more toward finicky family members than

durable individuals. There are some real princesses in this crew that mope unless given star treatment. I would never include most of the calatheas in the easy-does-it category. The only possible exception is the rattlesnake plant, *Calathea lancifolia*, but it gets brown leaf edges unless humidity is high. And who has those conditions at home during winter? Stick with marantas and ctenanthes. They have all the visual excitement anyone could ever desire, and they survive an occasional environmental insult without showing their disapproval. On that note, prayer plants fold their leaves at night, so don't panic when it happens. This is not body language for stress; your green roommate is just going to sleep.

Another point in marantas' favor is that you can find them at any supermarket. *Maranta leuconeura* (aka rabbit tracks because of its brown markings) and its offspring are available just about everywhere plants are sold. They are fairly compact, but they make an impressive presentation as they gain width. If a plant frequents supermarkets and big-box stores but still looks

For most prayer plants, the foliage is the main show. *Ctenanthe burlemarxii* 'Amagris' coming into blossom is downright thrilling, if subtleties send you.

like something you might want to adopt, it must be fairly impervious to abuse. Ctenanthes are not quite as omnipresent, but they are equally adaptable.

If you want to perk up your prayer plant, give it the bathroom treatment. All prayer plants respond to higher humidity than most homes furnish in the main living space. They like warm temperatures, but all (except the calatheas) seem to forgive my chilly reception. Do not forget to water them or you might court browning leaf edges. Flowers are not really a forte for this group of plants, but they are a nice touch. The exception is the never-never plant, *Ctenanthe oppenheimiana* 'Tricolor'. It has flaming red flower stalks that look something like bird-of-paradise spikes before they open. They match the equally bright red streaks running haphazardly through the leaves, and it's a snazzy package overall. Other prayer plants are not so well equipped with their accessories, but no matter: All eyes will be on the leaves.

PRAYER PLANT
Maranta and *Ctenanthe*

ALSO CALLED rabbit tracks, never-never plant
EASY

SIZE	Ranging from 6 to 24 inches (15 to 61 cm) high
FOLIAGE	Very jazzy and extremely diverse with stripes and streaks of color
OTHER ATTRIBUTES	Most don't have exciting flowers, but they're a cute addition
EXPOSURE	East or west
WATER REQUIREMENTS	Tends to be thirsty; keep the soil moderately moist and remember to repot so the roots aren't pot-bound
OPTIMUM NIGHTTIME TEMPERATURE	60–70°F (15–21°C)
RATE OF GROWTH	Slow to medium
SOIL TYPE	Humusy potting soil with compost included
FERTILIZING	Early spring to late autumn
ISSUES	Tends to be thirsty; avoid finicky calatheas in this group
COMPANIONS	Begonias, ferns, maidenhair vines, mosses, peperomias, plectranthus, and slipper orchids

RHIPSALIS

If you doubt that my tarantula-leg and sausage-link comparisons are on target, check out these two rhipsalis species.

f you like the look of spiders suspended from their webs, you are going to love rhipsalis. If you find hairy tarantula legs stirring, these plants are for you. And if you prefer all these kinky things coupled with an ironclad constitution, you are in luck. I've never met a rhipsalis that required more than just a pat and an occasional watering. Plus, they are all attractive—if spider associations don't give you the creepy-crawlies.

All rhipsalis have jointed stems with no perceptible leaves. The stems often bring to mind a series of tiny frankfurter links. *Rhipsalis baccifera* most closely resembles that image, while equally available *R. paradoxa* looks more like strings of crimped pasta. Some are furry (that's where the tarantula analogy comes in), while others are hairless. Those stems spill over the edge of the container and sprout groups of other stems, like a spider plant, but in more sophisticated fashion (my apologies to spider plant fans, but it is the truth). They have very small, cactus-like flowers (they are related to cacti) that look like little starbursts, but that perk occurs only in bright light. Following the blossoms you might even get round orbs of mistletoe-like berries. That's never happened for me, but I don't give it front-row seats in a south-facing window, which would be ideal. If you love the sound of this sort of package, you are not alone. There are rhipsalis collectors out there, judging from the entries in the Philadelphia Flower Show. I am not one of them, but I appreciate the plant. There's usually a rhipsalis or two hanging around my indoor garden. I don't know exactly how many are on the premises because they need no fuss.

As far as I know (again, I'm not an expert), all rhipsalis are easy to grow. I've never met a finicky member of this clan. I have run a few rhipsalis through endurance tests (forgetting to water, north-facing windows), and they've come out like heroes. The north-facing window led to some stretching stems that weren't as comely as the tighter versions grown in bright light, but that's the sum total of the fallout. And a stretchy stem on a rhipsalis doesn't look a whole lot different than the usual tight nest.

My biggest quandary with rhipsalis is dreaming up ways to make this out-of-the-ordinary plant really shine. Rhipsalis are usually sold in the typical litany of dowdy hanging plastic containers with their lax stems showering down. Not only does the look stray from my aesthetic, but I find it nearly impossible to host a hanger in my house. Watering a suspended plant always seems to lead to spills. And as mentioned earlier, coupling Einstein with a dangling plant is just asking for a crash. But although I've had rhipsalis plants for years, they've never needed anything beyond a regular pot. Perhaps fortunately, rhipsalis do not grow particularly quickly. This is an understatement: Their tufts of dangling stems are just

beginning to drape down after years in my fold. Eventually they'll graduate into tall cylinder-shaped pots to handle the draping foliage. Depending on your decor, you could go anywhere from sleek and ultra-modern to primitive or even woodsy.

You can place rhipsalis almost anywhere within the range of a light source. It tolerates very low light, and you could house it side by side with ferns. Begonias and African violets have a similar set of cultural preferences, and rhipsalis lends them an edge. On the other hand, if you want to go for flowers and fruit, giving your rhipsalis more sun would lead to a whole different set of companions in the succulent realm, and another mood entirely. Rhipsalis can be a game changer. They have a quirky attitude, which transfers to their roommates. Whoever is growing close by looks cool by association.

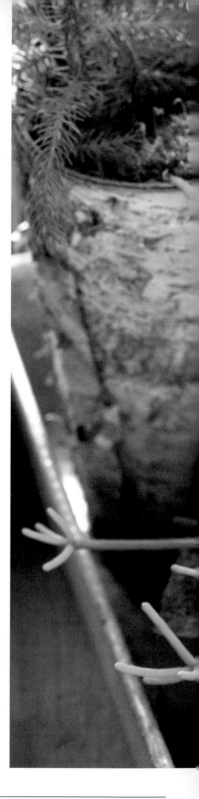

Growing *Rhipsalis baccifera* beside Norfolk Island pines evokes a sense of the forest, with all its creepy-crawlies included.

RHIPSALIS
Rhipsalis

ALSO CALLED old man's head, mistletoe cactus
EASIEST

SIZE	Sprawling
FOLIAGE	Think someone shrank hot dogs and hung them like suspended spiders
OTHER ATTRIBUTES	Can have starburst, cactus-like flowers and mistletoe-like berries
EXPOSURE	South is optimal if you want flowers and berries; even north has worked for me
WATER REQUIREMENTS	Allow soil to dry out between waterings
OPTIMUM NIGHTTIME TEMPERATURE	50–70°F (10–21°C)
RATE OF GROWTH	Slow
SOIL TYPE	Potting soil with sand and compost included
FERTILIZING	Early spring to late autumn
ISSUES	Gives some people the creepy-crawlies
COMPANIONS	In bright light can be coupled with succulents, aloes, agaves, euphorbias, and senecios; in lower light group with ferns, mosses, and Norfolk Island pines

SANSEVIERIA

I don't consider myself to be a plant snob. Want proof? I grow gladiolus in my outdoor garden. And I did dahlias when they were going through their déclassé stage. I even grow marigolds. But I admit that at one point I pooh-poohed sansevierias. I don't know why. Maybe I associated them with malls, greasy spoon diners, and dry cleaners.

All that has changed. Now I flip through catalogs in search of cool new spins on sansevierias. When I travel to far-flung places, I look for mom-and-pop greenhouses that might have a previously unseen sansevieria tucked into the woodwork. I even went to a botanical garden and asked to see the mother-in-law tongue collection. The beauty of this new fascination is that I can increase my inventory with the certain knowledge that any new acquisitions will not tax my workload. Sansevierias ask for nothing.

If sansevierias were once considered uncool, it was a brief event and a backlash against the fact that they were once omnipresent. Sansevierias are one of the few houseplants that are known by their Latin name, which indicates some measure of their appeal. I've been conducting informal surveys with lecture audiences, and these days not many people know them as mother-in-law's tongue (owing to the long-and-sharp association). As far as I'm concerned, it's time that snide remark was allowed to die. Another common name is snake plant, which is equally unendearing.

Some sansevierias do have barbs on their tips. They aren't as dangerous as those on agaves, which are in the same family, but they jut out like arrows and can definitely poke. Sansevierias thus armed can be a problem in the home. When Einstein was a kitten and prone to practicing his rocket-launching equipment (the Purrfessor has never really grasped the theory of gravity), I decided the barbed sansevierias could live only on the fireplace mantel, out of the path of any possible orbit. The fact that they are toxic also played a part in that decision, although Einstein learned immediately not to ingest any plant. He has grown out of his leaping stage, but I still clip the sharp tips off *Sansevieria cylindrica*. Dwarf rosette-forming *S. trifasciata* 'Hahnii' and its variations, of which I am particularly fond, have points on their tips, but they aren't sharp.

Chances are you've encountered one of the versions of *Sansevieria trifasciata* somewhere. Most often its long, spear-like stems are planted as a hedge or partition in an airport, shopping mall, or similar public space. You can be forgiven for overlooking it in your rush to take in the other scenery. Indeed, if anyone were to do the most-ignored-plant analysis, I bet snake plant would win hands down. But when sansevierias started their steady climb in the popularity polls,

new varieties started emerging. The *S.* 'Hahnii' contingent, with its tidy rosette of deep-green-and-golden striped leaves and many variations, is infinitely useful for covering the soil at the base of taller plants. It also makes a cute little accent all alone and is handy for places that might not be able to nurture anything else green. But I've also grown *S. trifasciata* 'Moonglow', which has broad matte silver leaves. The overall look is several notches above the standard fare, if not downright head turning. It's an excellent sentinel for a location that is not really capable of supporting most plant life. No matter how hot, dry, or dark the conditions, 'Moonglow' can take it. For the rare plant hound, there are several other sansevierias out there, including the painfully slow-growing *S. grandis*, which has thick, broad, speckled leaves that

pop up singly from the soil. It is a collector's item, but infinite patience is required to achieve a plant that will allow you to boast rather than issue a disclaimer ("Honestly, one day it will not look like it came from a demolition site").

Sansevierias are not usually grown for their flowers, but blossoms have been known to happen on some varieties (and since most sansevierias are hand-me-downs, few people can identify them by name). When they do occur, the flowers are white, small, fluffy, and sometimes headily fragrant.

As for care, they are all bulletproof. I have never met anyone who has killed a sansevieria. It's nearly impossible to do. A lot of people have thrown them out, but few have succeeded in neglecting them to death. If you want to do it right, give sansevierias indirect light (they can burn in a direct south-facing window), water them when the soil is dry (which happens often if you haven't repotted), and provide average home temperatures. Humidity, or lack thereof, is not usually an issue. When they are happy (and it doesn't take much to please them), sansevierias will increase by sending up more snakes. They do this with so much gusto that they have been known to muscle out of plastic containers, so move your sansevieria into a clay pot as soon as possible. Select a container that is squat and weighty on the bottom; the crowd of heavy succulent leaves can topple easily. Another solution is to divide off some of the leaves. Surely you know some folks who desperately need a plant they cannot possibly kill, try though they might.

SANSEVIERIA
Sansevieria

ALSO CALLED **mother-in-law's tongue, snake plant**
EASIEST

SIZE	Ranging from 6 to 20 inches (15 to 50 cm) high, depending on the variety
FOLIAGE	Forming a plump rosette in some, tall and lean in others; some have wonderful markings
OTHER ATTRIBUTES	Tolerates near-death experiences
EXPOSURE	Almost anywhere that has some sort of light source
WATER REQUIREMENTS	Allow soil to dry out between waterings; will tolerate a lot of forgetfulness
OPTIMUM NIGHTTIME TEMPERATURE	50–70°F (10–21°C)
RATE OF GROWTH	Slow to medium
SOIL TYPE	Humusy potting soil with compost included
FERTILIZING	Unnecessary; if you feel the urge, early spring to late autumn
ISSUES	Can muscle out of its container; repot into clay or something that can't be cracked easily
COMPANIONS	Just about any plant; I love to couple the tall ones with nerve plants and polka dot plants or creeping fig

A HITCHHIKER'S GUIDE TO DIVIDING OFF

Sansevierias aren't the only plants that push the limits and multiply when they're happy. Many individuals in this book make progeny when they are treated well. You could leave them in their containers and let them duke it out, or you could give them a graduation into a larger pot and hope they all live in peace and harmony. Another solution is to divide off the pups and share the wealth. With most of these plants, it's easy.

Agaves, aloes, carex, haworthias, and hens and chicks are prime targets for division. But don't be too hasty to share. Wait for a plant to make a full rosette before you take the axe to it. In most cases it's obvious when the little flock of pups begins to form. When the progeny start to look like their parents, they're usually ripe for potting alone.

Here's how to do it: First, water the plant and wait an hour or so for the water to percolate down. Then remove the pot, exposing the soil and root ball. Examine the plant and make sure the plantlets have their own healthy root systems. This is critical. If they don't appear to have separate roots for sustenance, wait until they do before dividing them off. If they have their own roots, carefully untangle those roots from the parent plant and pull (or cut) the pup from its parent. Pot it alone in its own container, taking care to match the receiving vessel with its root system. When repotting the parent plant, be sure to fill soil into the empty spot the plantlet has vacated. Finally, water them both. It's as easy as that. Pretty soon you'll be mighty popular with other potential houseplant gardeners.

SCHEFFLERA

Until you start playing with it, you wouldn't think *Schefflera arboricola* would have what it takes to mesh with modern surroundings. But this sleek presentation proves that scheffleras can be swank.

wasn't sure I liked schef-fleras. In fact, I was pretty sure they left me cold. The plant just didn't have enough going on. But then I found a perfect container—a modern little number in whitewashed porcelain—that just needed drainage holes. Meanwhile, I met a small schefflera that needed a great setting. A match was made.

Sometimes that's the way indoor gardening comes together. In fact, it is how interior decor generally occurs around here. Odd components meet in my mind's eye, I make the introduction, and they end up spending their lives together while improving my happy home. Maybe a container with a totally different look would be equally snazzy, but that can happen when promotion time rolls around.

And promotions are definitely a possibility for schef-fleras. Eventually they become large and often gangly, but that takes years. Of course, this plant will likely remain part of your family for the foreseeable future, maybe longer. But a schef-flera looks most endearing in its juvenile stage, when the leaves resemble little finger-like segments radiating from a central rib. One of its most descriptive common names is octopus tree, which might give you a working image. The schefflera of my youth was most commonly *Schef-flera actinophylla*, which has a more open habit. Nowa-days you are more apt to find the neater, tighter *S. arboricola* on the market. The leaves are shiny, dark green, and vaguely Asian looking. They also come in variegated versions with irregular streaks or edging. No matter which way you go, the whole vision is fairly swank.

A schefflera seems most congruous in a modern set-ting, although it takes on all sorts of roles. I've seen the plant loitering around Victorian parlors and looking like it belonged in an ornate container. I took the sleek, modern approach and liked the composite picture just fine. But I might go one step further. A schefflera is often tucked singly into a corner, but a mini grove of schef-fleras could read like a little dell right there in your home. If you mix the plain green version with its variegated kin, the result will read like a group of andromedas.

Say what you will about scheffleras—and feel free to yawn—but this plant is dura-ble, it will become sizable, and it is always neatly clad. It has no pouting, dropping leaves; it is always wearing a shiny dark green outfit in a small shrub presentation. My schefflera came as a few plants potted together. That cluster works well toward bringing in a nice symmetrical unit, but communal living also leads to a thirstier customer. It dries out a few times a week, especially when the furnace is running, but that hasn't put a crimp in its positive attitude. The beauty of a schef-flera is that it doesn't voice any disgruntlement when you forget it. Over the long run it's not going to like constant neglect, but you would have to ignore it on a regular basis to bring on a mutiny. And there's no harm in pruning back a schefflera; it will (eventually) make side branches to fill out. You could divide up multiple bedfellows and still achieve a well-rounded result.

Not many plants can give you the stature that a schefflera achieves indoors without a whole lot of hassle. And scheffleras really need next to nothing besides water (and they forgive some transgressions with your drink-serving schedule). Mine is growing on the dining room table with only indirect light. It's slightly one-sided in its pursuit of better sunbeams, but aside from that it's doing just fine. Someday I'll repot it and coax it along the path toward a chunkier shrub. But in the meantime I'm really beginning to like this plant. It's growing on me.

SCHEFFLERA
Schefflera

ALSO CALLED **octopus tree**
EASIEST

SIZE	Will remain less than 12 inches (30 cm) high for quite a while before growing into a small shrub
FOLIAGE	Leaves come in sets of fingers from the stem; several varieties are variegated
OTHER ATTRIBUTES	Just a nice, tidy plant
EXPOSURE	East or west work best
WATER REQUIREMENTS	Keep soil moderately moist
OPTIMUM NIGHTTIME TEMPERATURE	50–65°F (10–18°C)
RATE OF GROWTH	Slow
SOIL TYPE	Rich, humusy potting soil with compost included
FERTILIZING	Early spring to late autumn
PROPAGATION	By cuttings, but woody rooting hormone might be helpful
ISSUES	Can become a leggy specimen, but pruning will solve that. *Caution! The ASPCA lists schefflera among the most toxic plants to pets*
COMPANIONS	African violets, bromeliads, false aralia, ivies, mosses, nerve plants, peperomias, and pileas

SENECIO

It's easy to find the indestructible branch of the senecio family. Look for the succulent types, like *Senecio articulata* (top left), S. *cephalophorus* 'Blazin' Glory' (top right), and S. *rowleyanus* (lower).

don't want to lead you astray. There are a whole lot of senecios out there, and not all of them are indestructible. But some are real troupers indoors, and they deserve a place in these pages.

Before you break into a cold sweat, there is an easy shortcut for identifying some of the simpler senecios to host indoors: Seek out the succulent lookalikes. If a senecio has foliage that mimics a succulent, there is a good chance it can share your hospitality without becoming a nuisance. Some sterling examples are blue chalksticks, *Senecio serpens*, with tall stems clad in what look like blue-gray icicles; string of pearls, S. *rowleyanus*, which has long thread-like stems holding a necklace of round beads; S. *citriformis*, which is similar to string of pearls but with citrus pip-shaped beads; and S. *cephalophorus* 'Blazin' Glory', with long silver leaves dusted in a powdery farina and topped by paintbrush-like orange blossoms. Most of these senecios go way back in my history as a houseplant

hound, but I discovered 'Blazin' Glory' only recently. I was so pleased with this plant before I had any inkling that flowers were in its future that I gave it prime billing in my window display. When it began to produce a crop of chubby silver buds, I was thrilled. Then the flowers burst open into their bright orange brush and my pulse really began to quicken.

Paintbrush-like blossoms are a common trait for many senecios. Unfortunately, they aren't always as glam as those on 'Blazin' Glory'. In fact, they usually look like a dandelion when it's beginning to set seeds. When the flowers are white and blah (which can be the case with senecios), they're often a distraction and might best be removed—especially if they smell like gym socks, which can happen. But the paintbrush characteristic helps distinguish them from the other members of the daisy family.

Another pleasant surprise was dusty miller (*Senecio cineraria*). You've probably seen it in window boxes or flower arrangements. Dusty

miller has thick silver-white leaves that are deeply segmented and resemble those on an artemisia. It makes a great houseplant, as I discovered one recent autumn when I moved it inside while struggling not to sacrifice my plants to frost.

Dusty miller proved to be a delight, but it wasn't exactly a diehard. The plant is a little thirstier than its carefree kin. But if you give it plenty of root room, the leaves won't curl up, which is its body language for reminding you to stop by soon with the watering pot. If you forget to water, it bounces back. You get a few second chances.

I'm also keen on *Senecio macroglossus* 'Variegatus', another unlikely relative in a family full of dissimilarities. This energetic trailing plant sends waxy hexagonal leaves wandering around like an ivy; in fact, one common name is natal ivy. The leaves are glossy with creamy margins, and the plant has a variegated holly appearance. With a little finesse it wouldn't be a bad plant for winter holiday displays.

It's a broad generalization,

but senecios with nonsucculent growth and daisy-like flowers can be a bear indoors. Florist's cineraria (formerly called *Senecio hybrid* and newly classified as *Pericallis hybrida*) is hawked as a charming windowsill performer when Easter rolls around because of its slam-bang flowers in bright shades. But trust me, it's a pill. It attracts aphids and whitefly like a magnet. Steer clear.

Now that I've laid out all the odd fellows in this family, how would you show them off? You might want to give blue chalksticks, *Senecio serpens*, showstopper billing. I planted mine in a cobalt blue glazed long Tom, and even though it is pitted against a crowd of other plants, people halt in their tracks to admire it. Pair it with *S. cephalophorus* 'Blazin' Glory' and both will shine to their best advantage. If you throw in a few seashells or kinky artifacts, you will have a museum-quality exhibition.

Trailing senecios, such as string of pearls, *Senecio rowleyanus*, and *S. citriformis*, can serve as a ground cover below another plant that loves a bright window and regular watering. Although senecios look like succulents, they tend to dry out frequently. I let them dangle down from a pedestal urn or another container that allows them to shower. Again, remember to water the plant regularly, as pedestal planters tend to have great drainage. In the right setting, all senecios can grow lush. For *S. rowleyanus* and its lookalikes, that can mean curtains of beads sufficient to make any disco dancer's eyes light up. If the go-go feels a little dated to you, give it an updated swing. So far, Einstein has not discovered the thrill of batting the beads around. But that day will surely come.

Planted in a cobalt pot, blue chalksticks (*Senecio serpens*) really stands out, especially when underplanted with *Iresine* 'Purple Lady'.

Senecio rowleyanus looks just like its nickname, string of pearls.

SENECIO

Senecio

ALSO CALLED blue chalksticks (*Senecio serpens*), string of pearls (*S. rowleyanus*)
EASIEST

SIZE	24 inches (61 cm) high for blue chalksticks; others dangle down
FOLIAGE	Very diverse, but the succulent-like versions are the most indestructible
OTHER ATTRIBUTES	Some have racy flowers; most are grown for their strange leaves
EXPOSURE	South is optimal; east or west can also work
WATER REQUIREMENTS	Allow soil to dry out between waterings, but that can happen frequently
OPTIMUM NIGHTTIME TEMPERATURE	50–65°F (10–18°C)
RATE OF GROWTH	Medium to fast
SOIL TYPE	Rich, humusy potting soil with compost included
FERTILIZING	Early spring to late autumn
PROPAGATION	By cuttings; *Senecio rowleyanus* often has aerial roots that make cuttings easy
ISSUES	*Senecio serpens* can break off stems easily as it adds weight
COMPANIONS	Companions: Iresine, mirror plants, spider plants, succulents, and tradescantia

SILVER SQUILL

Diehard plants can do stunts, and that's how this never-say-die silver squill (*Ledebouria socialis*) got tucked into a tackle box with a haworthia and mini jade plant, then top-dressed with marbles.

'm coming through the door, hauling my usual load of booty snagged at a flea market. After a few trips back and forth to the Volvo, a little mountain of what other people would classify as junk has accumulated in the greenhouse. Einstein is checking for any suspicious scents on the tackle box, Bundt mold, colander, sieves, and wooden tool caddy I scored this week. Meanwhile, I have no idea what I'm going to do with any of it, until out of the corner of my eye I see the silver squill.

I don't always go the wacky route when repotting. Most often I find a fitting terracotta container and house my plant in it. But occasionally I get the urge to go crazy, and that's when I hit the flea markets. I rarely have a plan. When proprietors ask if I'm looking for something specific, I just flash the *Babes in Toyland* look and shake my dazed head. I simply collect cool stuff that speaks to me and wait for inspiration to strike. But plants like silver squill allow me to put my flea market treasures to work.

Silver squill, *Ledebouria socialis* and once known as *Scilla violacea*, is a funky little pass-along plant with the type of legendary fortitude necessary to make the leap into recycled funkware. It's not easy to describe. Imagine a little aboveground pip-shaped burgundy bulb about 1 to 2 inches long (2.5 to 5 cm). From the top of that bulb, succulent silver leaves sprout splattered with irregular green scale-like markings. The aboveground bulbs congregate in little clutches, hence the *socialis* part of the binomial. More often than not, an arched wand of minute pink-cream nodding flowers caps the units. The whole package is slightly reminiscent of grape hyacinths (minus the azure blue), which are related. To give you a feeling for the ambiance, a toad would look perfectly comfortable in close company with a silver squill.

Why does my tackle box (or whatever it is) bring silver squill to mind? When you're working with unconventional containers, it's best to pair them with ultra-adaptable plants. And sure

enough, after I drilled drainage holes in the bottom of the tackle box, the squill settled in happily to resume its steady business of surrounding itself with more little bulbous companions. The silver in the leaves is a natural with any metal container. In fact, the whole demeanor of the plant lends itself to offbeat presentations. Because of its small dimensions, the composition is not going to call to someone from across the room, but it is apt to provoke a smile up close. I keep it in the bathroom, where people have time to sit and ponder. I figure it's a good fit with *Farmers' Almanac*.

Best of all, silver squill is infinitely adaptable. It is cool with the ultra-humid, damp, poorly lit atmosphere in a terrarium as well as a xerophytic, very dry, sunny situation. Will it croak because of lack of humidity in midwinter? Definitely not. Will it perish if you leave it outdoors beside a downspout? Probably not, although some bulbs might wash away. I grow silver squill anywhere. My south-facing windows are prime real estate reserved for

Silver squill is definitely a funky plant—tiny but memorable.

plants that must have bright light, so silver squill doesn't usually get that royal treatment, even though the plant might love it. Instead, I give ledebouria an east- or west-facing position, and it is fine. North might even work in a pinch. I water them when the soil is dry; the bulbs can store moisture to keep for reserves. And I play with it whenever the opportunity arises. The good news about silver squill is that it can generally spare a few bulbs to begin new colonies. It's a great plant for making converts.

SILVER SQUILL
Ledebouria socialis

EASIEST

SIZE	3 inches (7 cm) high
FOLIAGE	Silver with irregular green markings above little colonies of bulbs
OTHER ATTRIBUTES	Small curlicues of lily-of-the-valley-like pink blossoms
EXPOSURE	South is optimal, but east or west is also fine; could probably tolerate north in a pinch
WATER REQUIREMENTS	Allow soil to dry out between waterings
OPTIMUM NIGHTTIME TEMPERATURE	50–65°F (10–18°C)
RATE OF GROWTH	Medium
SOIL TYPE	Rich, humusy potting soil with compost included
FERTILIZING	Early spring to late autumn
PROPAGATION	Divide off the little bulbs when they've initiated their own roots
ISSUES	None
COMPANIONS	Hens and chicks, mirror plants, polka dot plants, rhipsalis, and senecios

SLIPPER ORCHID

Although this slipper orchid, *Paphiopedilum maudiae*, doesn't blossom in summer, it reliably reblooms in winter and the flower holds its pristine condition for months.

rchids, indestructible? If you doubt these two words can ever be said together, you have never tried a tropical slipper orchid. Mine is less bother than your average goldfish. Actually, I should use the plural, as over the years I have amassed quite a collection of tropical slipper orchids. I cannot resist these charming elf-faced flowers during the duration of their prolonged bloom stint, which continues for many months. Once you have a paphiopedilum, it's a keeper. If you can patiently host it during the time when flowers are not in the cards—that is, most of the summer—chances are good that you will see blossom spikes developing sometime in late autumn and throughout winter. I know most orchids have the reputation for being prima donnas that require an emerald green thumb, but paphiopedilum is the exception. If you give it a chance in your home, I promise you won't regret it.

Not only is this orchid painless, but it will also be one of your triumphs. The blossoms put on a leisurely, graceful presentation starting from a goose-necked bud that has one of the most seductively slow windups you will ever experience. Waiting for a tropical lady's slipper to open will leave you panting in anticipation. By the time the flower begins to unfurl, you will be mopping the brow of your great expectations. And tropical lady's slippers never disappoint. The art-installation-caliber blossoms are 3 inches (7 cm) in diameter and easily seen from a distance. They are the stuff of poetry. *Paphiopedilum maudiae* group is the easiest of the easies. The flowers are cream with pale green stripes, and they look like grinning elves complete with caps. The beauty of this particular group is that the foliage has dark green mottling over a paler green base, giving you something to enjoy while waiting for the main show. If you want something flashier, there are plenty of lady's slippers with parrot green and burgundy flowers. But lady's slippers have the standard-fare green orchid foliage that is thick and sprouting from the base.

A close second to paphiopedilum is moth orchid, phalaenopsis. At one time you could not open an interior decorating magazine without spotting a moth orchid lurking somewhere in a photograph. I envisioned stylists driving around with a moth orchid in the passenger seat, a constant companion ready to jump into any picture. Any living thing that can be dragged around to this extent is bound to be a survivor.

The only challenge connected with a moth orchid is achieving repeat bloom. But future flowers are just gravy because the first string of blossoms is sufficient to make a purchase totally worthwhile. When a moth orchid blooms, expect to be thrilled nonstop for several months as each flower on the spike unfolds. The full-size versions might have four or five blossoms, each 3 inches (7 cm) wide, looking like a swarm of moths ascending. But the new cool is the miniature introductions with three to four flowers about the size of a quarter. And the color range has gone far beyond the original pure white flowers to include pinks and reds with stripes and dapples. The biggest thrill is the boasting rights. You can be a rank beginner and still croon about your bounty of orchid blossoms.

Where many people get shaky with orchids is the growing medium. Although orchids are grown in everything from Styrofoam noodles to pebbles, mixing Coco-chips (they come as a brick that you soak in water) with about a tablespoon of horticultural charcoal works for me. The most difficult part of the process is freeing the orchid from its original container because the roots tend to adhere to the sides. When you loosen it from the plastic pot in which it was purchased, the previous medium will probably fall from the roots. Just spread the newly liberated roots out in a new container. I usually go about twice the size of the original pot. Tuck the Coco-chip–charcoal medium around the roots, making sure to bury them.

Because of my room-for-one-more houseplant policy, I rarely bring my population explosion to the sink for watering, but I make an exception for the orchids. I grow mine on plant stands in the bathroom, close to the sink. Every three to four days I bring them to the sink, let water run through the bark, and allow the pot to drain for a couple of minutes before returning it to the plant stand. The sieve action is fine with these orchids, because that's the sort of treatment they enjoy in their home jungles. The bathroom is also ducky because it is the warmest room in my chilly house, and they prefer to grow at 65°F (18°C) for daytime temperatures with just a slight dip at night. My morning shower also raises their humidity. The bathroom faces east, which is ideal for an orchid, although I keep them away from the panes because they burn easily in bright light. If your bathroom windows are otherwise monopolized (or nonexistent), consider running a humidifier or using a pebble tray to increase the humidity in other parts of the house. This will make them happier, but high humidity is not a deal-breaker for these particular orchids. In fact, tropical lady's slippers and moth orchids are delightfully congenial. They make champions of us all.

SLIPPER ORCHID
Paphiopedilum cultivars
EASY

SIZE	Leaves are about 5 inches (12 cm), with flower spikes that generally shoot up 12 to 18 inches (30 to 45 cm) high
FOLIAGE	Generally dark green; *Paphiopedilum maudiae* has pale green leaves with irregular darker green markings
OTHER ATTRIBUTES	Long-lasting large, graceful flowers
EXPOSURE	East or west; can burn in bright light
WATER REQUIREMENTS	Water once every 3 to 4 days by letting water run through the medium
OPTIMUM NIGHTTIME TEMPERATURE	Prefers temperatures that do not fall below 60°F (15°C) at night
RATE OF GROWTH	Very slow
SOIL TYPE	Coco-chips mixed with a tablespoon of horticultural charcoal
FERTILIZING	Early spring to late autumn
ISSUES	Can be difficult to repot, but it's a piece of cake once you get the hang of it
COMPANIONS	African violets, begonias, hoyas, and other plants that like warmth and indirect light

SNOW ROSE

The variegated snow rose, *Serissa foetida* 'Mount Fuji', looks like a tiny boxwood plant, with the perk of minute white flowers.

This little plant tried so hard to be included in the book, so I couldn't leave it out. You wouldn't believe the obstacle course the snow rose completed to receive diehard status. It's one of the smaller packages in my green menagerie, so sometimes the watering can passes blindly over it without depositing a drop. Did it flinch? No. Sometimes it didn't get a prime light location. Did it croak? Never. If the negligence continued for a few weeks, its tiny pinky-nail-size leaves shriveled, but they remained intact and held firmly to the woody stems. And when I remembered to water and gave it a better seat in the house, the plant gratefully burst into pristine white flowers that look like someone shrank the rose. So why did I hesitate before adding *Serissa foetida* to the table of contents? It's not readily available. Obscurity is its only fault.

Perhaps if I shout out its praises, the big-box stores will pay heed and stock it. Until then you'll have to ferret it out from specialty nurseries. Grab it if you can. Snow rose is impeccably tidy, very intriguing, and congenial beyond belief. It's also a dead ringer for a little tree. Grow this plant as a bonsai, or just keep it around to admire its petite dimensions without having to clip and shear. The tiny, glossy deep green leaves appear sparsely on the woody stems. For an extra thrill, go for a variegated version with a distinct white margin and midrib streak, such as 'Mount Fuji'. It's cute even when it isn't blooming, and I've seen it trained into a miniature espalier, which is enough to speed your pulse (and win you a prize at the flower show). Then come the flowers, which appear at pretty much any time of year. In early spring my snow rose is in full blossom after a winter of semi-neglect but not discontent. The single version has five-petal flowers tucked into the tips of the branches, sort of like mini oxalis blossoms. If that's not enough, there's a double version, 'Flore Pleno', with white flowers that really do look like minute rosebuds—hence the name snow rose. A whisper pink version is also available.

Snow rose is a slow-growing plant, which may explain why it hasn't caught the eye of the mass-production industry. Years might come and go before it makes a whole lot of growth. Eventually it has the potential to look like a boxwood indoors. And wouldn't it be fun to have an orb-like evergreen inside to remind you of your favorite garden scenes? Multiples of the plant might be wonderful accents in front of matching windows in a traditional living room, if given good light. You can train it into any shape you adore. Let the Zen begin.

Give a serissa the good life and provide ample root room. Don't try to cram the roots into a tiny container; a roomy pot will reduce stress and make life easier for the poor wee thing. My snow rose is very thirsty, which is another reason I occasionally neglect to keep up with its watering needs. It would love a south-facing window, but if all you have is east or west, that's fine. You could fiddle around with fine-tuning its shape or just let it assume its natural form. Either way, it's going to stay petite for the foreseeable future. But that's what we love about it.

SNOW ROSE
Serissa foetida
EASY

SIZE	Remains less than 6 inches (15 cm) high for a long time before becoming a small bush
FOLIAGE	Very tiny, about the size of a plump rice grain, sometimes with silver markings
OTHER ATTRIBUTES	Has tiny oxalis-like flowers; the double version looks like minute rosebuds
EXPOSURE	South, east, or west
WATER REQUIREMENTS	Keep soil moderately moist; bounces back from wilts, but don't overdo the punishment
OPTIMUM NIGHTTIME TEMPERATURE	55–65°F (12–18°C)
RATE OF GROWTH	Slow
SOIL TYPE	Rich, humusy potting soil with compost included
FERTILIZING	Early spring to late autumn
ISSUES	Slow-growing
COMPANIONS	Geraniums, iresine, plectranthus, and rhipsalis

KEEPING MINIATURE PLANTS DIMINUTIVE

We live in a society where bigger is usually seen as better. We rank our achievement by how huge we can grow things. But not all houseplant gardeners have the window space to host immense plants. If you want to keep your houseplants in check, focus on those that are likely to stay small. There are plenty in this book. Consider an African violet, haworthia, hens and chicks, miniature ivy, moss, peperomia, rhipsalis, silver squill, or snow rose. Many succulents also remain compact.

If you want a diminutive plant that won't take up much of your valuable window space, the path of least resistance is to select something that has the dimensions you prefer without requiring a lot of surgery. But even if you go with small plants, many of them—like the snow rose—will benefit from some constructive training.

Feel free to wield pruning shears frequently and with conviction. The more you work with a plant, the better it will look. Pruning is a beauty treatment for your houseplants. Sculpt that plant and it will gain a personality. Before you start, give the whole plant a quick assessment and think about your goal. Do you want a round orb shape? Would you prefer an open-branched bonsai appearance? Are you just striving to maintain the status quo? Make your clips thoughtfully.

When you prune a plant, always cut as close as possible above a leaf so no naked stems are left. Shear off leggy growth, especially shoots that have initiated in low light. Strive to coax a plant to become all it can be

Another strategy is to be a little stingy with fertilizer. It can be a delicate balance between starving your green roommate and merely keeping it on a diet. Do not exceed the instructions on your plant food label, and consider fertilizing less frequently than recommended. Along the same lines, don't grant container promotions too liberally, and let the roots become slightly cramped. This strategy can also be tricky, because you don't want the plant to dry out continually. But if a plant isn't wilting between waterings, wait with the pot promotions. Your plant will fit into a niche that is comfortable in your home over the long haul. A little plant can go a long way.

SPIDER PLANT

Until recently I wouldn't let a spider plant through the door. Now *Chlorophytum comosum* 'Bonnie' is one of my favorite plants in the house.

I had to overcome an attitude toward spider plants. Originally this was going to be an all-indestructibles-except-spider-plants book. But then I met *Chlorophytum comosum* 'Bonnie'.

Before 'Bonnie', I didn't think there was hope for spider plants. To me they always looked like a variegated grass hit by a lightning bolt gone viral. And if one *Chlorophytum comosum* wasn't bad enough, it cloned itself a few dozen times to produce a population explosion of little progeny. People are prone to take off the little spiders and foist them on innocent souls. Not in my house. You can harbor plants that look like a bad hair day, but I won't be a willing accomplice. I don't care how easy they are to cultivate. At least, that was my line in the past.

Then a friend introduced me to 'Bonnie', and I threw all my prejudices right out the window. 'Bonnie' has lots of white-striped leaves, but they form a nifty twisting-turning maelstrom. Instead of sending out lank spiders, 'Bonnie' shoots curly runners that hold a series of twisted sisters. Who would have dreamed?

But the saga doesn't end there. If I stuffed 'Bonnie' into a smudged white hanging basket and let it sway precariously from a curtain rod (just begging Einstein to try out his Tarzan moves), I would have liked the plant as much as I like any plain Jane chlorophytum—that is, not at all. I had to find it the right package, and one trip to the local vintage store did it. For $12, I came home with the perfect milky white, matte-finish, pedestal Floraline vase.

As with any spider plant, 'Bonnie' is no trouble whatsoever. All spider plants can tend toward thirsty, with their bulk of foliage to quench. But if I forget to water 'Bonnie' frequently, no pouting results. I fertilize the plant, but there are no perceptible repercussions if I forget. Proof again that treating a spider plant like a queen leads to the same results as treating a spider plant like a spider plant.

Just a note about the air-purifying action of

houseplants. I'll put up a good argument in support of any plant's ability to make your home environment healthier. But scientists have tested a slew of popular foliage plants for their air-purifying abilities. In a NASA study, first place went to peace lilies (*Spathiphyllum*). Spider plants were the runner-up. I contend that less-known plants could have received similar high marks if they had been tested. But the fact that a spider plant quickly produces a major wad of foliage is a big plus in its favor. It makes air purification easy. Indeed, most of the plants in the NASA study—including many of the hard hitters in this book, such as Chinese evergreen (*Aglaonema*), pothos (*Epipremnum*), philodendron, ivy (*Hedera helix*), and fig (*Ficus*)—got great rankings. That's just one more good reason to drop your attitude and embrace houseplants. Give that plant your best shot. Ponder how to incorporate it into your decor, and then display it with all the creativity you can muster. Keep it groomed and gorgeous. Any plant can be beautiful if you give it a chance. I'm even thinking of dividing off some runners from my 'Bonnie', making multiple plants to display, and sharing. Want one?

SPIDER PLANT
Chlorophytum comosum
EASIEST

SIZE	A large unit overall, but 'Bonnie' grows slower than the typical spider plant; all drape down
FOLIAGE	Long, thin, and grass-like, with white streaks; 'Bonnie' has curly leaves
OTHER ATTRIBUTES	Forms a series of spiders showering down
EXPOSURE	Just about any window works; I do east or west
WATER REQUIREMENTS	Tends to be thirsty, but doesn't mind a little forgetfulness
OPTIMUM NIGHTTIME TEMPERATURE	50–70°F (10–21°C)
RATE OF GROWTH	Fast
SOIL TYPE	Humusy potting soil with compost included
FERTILIZING	Early spring to late autumn; won't pout if you forget
ISSUES	Keep it neatly groomed!
COMPANIONS	Aglaonemas, begonias, crotons, dracaenas, ferns, ficus, ivies, mosses, nerve plants, peperomias, and polka dot plants

LEVITATING SPRAWLING PLANTS

A hanging plant is probably the most cumbersome of all configurations to host in the average home. Who needs a plant you can't reach with the watering can? Who wants the inevitable spills when you try to take aim with a spout? No one likes mounting a ladder every time a plant needs water. Hanging plants tend to be neglected. Don't do that to yourself and your green buddies.

I use tall containers to cradle plants that tend to drape down. This works like a charm. I engage long Torus or pedestal pots, and I've even enlisted florist buckets for the purpose. Umbrella stands will do the job. They all give the plant an opportunity to trail down without increasing the footprint of the container.

People often ask if I fill my tall containers completely with potting soil. Absolutely yes. I never use packing noodles, crumpled newspaper, or any other type of filler to take up the lower space below the root ball. And I inflict the same graduation process that I follow with all plants. I don't put a little cutting into a very deep container; I start in a smaller pot and then move it up. I take care to water the plant often enough that the water seeps down and keeps the roots quenched even though the mouth is not gaping. On the other hand, I don't overwater when the plant is newly potted into a container with lots of soil waiting for the roots to plunge down.

The end result can be riveting. Some of my favorite plants are trailers, and they make a strong and unique statement. A pedestal container elevated a spider plant in my estimation. That was a major accomplishment.

TRADESCANTIA

Tradescantia brings me back. The inch plant runs through all the nascent memories of the many houseplants I met early in the game. I was only a teenager when I first fell in love with Logee's Greenhouses, the place where my budding interest in horticulture initially laid down roots and flourished. Before that, I mostly favored marigolds, tulips, and hyacinths stuffed into suburban foundation plantings. But I got deep into it at Logee's. My recollections are dominated by 100-year-old Ponderosa lemons, mammoth kumquat trees, and massive camellias. But weaving those highlights together is the little inch plant that found a home in the greenhouses more than fifty years before I arrived and could be found lurking in nooks off the beaten track. (Logee's had plenty of hidden scenic detours where little jogs off the aisles could lead you into wonderful tangles with groping vines and creeping tropicals.)

The plant encountered in those thickets of jungle-under-glass was *Tradescantia fluminensis*, probably one of the least exciting of the clan, with small, cheerful shiny green leaves along fast-moving stems. You could weed this plant out in gobs and come back the next week to find another few fistfuls. The joke was that it grew an inch every night, and another common name is speedy Henry. Recently speedy Henry has become even more racy. Now there are variegated versions, plus one with pink streaks in the foliage. They strike me as tarted-up versions of the old faithful. But whether you want to go with the party animal or the plain vanilla, aside from pruning and a slight tendency to get whitefly, all are absolutely carefree.

My *Tradescantia fluminensis* memories are entangled with another close relative. bridal veil, *Gibasis geniculata*, classified at one time as *Tradescantia multiflora*. Bridal veil has slender, pointed leaves at regular intervals on lax, jointed stems. As you might imagine from the name, it produces a veil of tiny white blossoms, almost like baby's breath.

Both plants are rooted deep in gardening traditions, but I recommend white velvet, *Tradescantia sillamontana*. This robust plant is indomitable but also ravishingly beautiful. It fits better with a more modern milieu. It is swank, with thick, succulent leaves covered in a hoar of fleece. It can tolerate really low light. If you give it bright sunshine, it grows faster into a tight mass of creeping leaves and has an overall tidier appearance than the light-lacking edition. But it doesn't meander all over the place no matter what sort of conditions you provide. Instead, it just gets denser. And then pink flowers appear nestled in the tips, playing fetchingly off the white fuzz. In terms of drinking, it's like a succulent—feel free to forget it once in a while.

I'm also fond of *Tradescantia zebrina*. It was strongly associated with the psychedelic era, but only for its far-out metallic silver-and-purple striped leaves (a deep violet streak runs down the center of each leaf, while a pair of purple stripes lines the edges). You could stuff a handful of this plant into your macramé hanging basket, and it would root in a blink and be dangling down to the flare in your bell-bottoms in no time. And in the days when we were forever headed to the next sit-down strike, who had a minute to water? *Tradescantia zebrina* is cool with lapses in care. It gets a little hairy when you forget to prune, but I keep it in check. I still grow *T. zebrina* as a ground cover below other plants, but I no longer use it as a stand-alone specimen. And I got over macramé many moons ago.

Equally colorful and thoroughly modern is *Tradescantia spathacea*, formerly known as *Rhoeo spathacea* and also called Moses in the bulrushes (plus Moses in his cradle, men in a boat, and oyster plant). The original version—nothing to sneeze at—was adorned by green leaves on the upper surface with pink-burgundy below. Rather than dangling down, it forms elongated rosettes rising from the base that give it a more buttoned-down look. But the plant spin doctors added some additional

Planting it alone feels outdated, so I use *Tradescantia zebrina* in tandem with something else. Here it's coupled with *Oxalis triangularis* 'Charmed Wine'.

TRADESCANTIA
Tradescantia

ALSO CALLED inch plant, bridal veil, Moses in the bulrushes, Moses in his cradle, men in a boat, oyster plant

EASIEST

SIZE	Almost all are trailing plants, except Moses in the bulrushes, which stands less than 6 inches (15 cm) high
FOLIAGE	Very variable but usually colorful; generally on trailing stems
OTHER ATTRIBUTES	Some versions have flowers, but the blossoms are rarely the highlight
EXPOSURE	East or west is fine; not necessary to grow it directly in a window
WATER REQUIREMENTS	Can tolerate very wet conditions, but it isn't necessary to water often, as it rarely wilts
OPTIMUM NIGHTTIME TEMPERATURE	50–70°F (10–21°C)
RATE OF GROWTH	Very fast
SOIL TYPE	Humusy potting soil with compost included
FERTILIZING	Early spring to late autumn; won't pout if you forget
ISSUES	Be vigilant with your pruning shears; can look untidy quickly
COMPANIONS	Aglaonemas, begonias, crotons, dracaenas, ferns, ficus, ivies, mosses, nerve plants, peperomias, and polka dot plants

icing on the cake. Newbie 'Golden Oyster' has amber leaves etched by green pinstripes and red undersides. This stunner makes a great window box, or you can use it below other plants to hide their soil. Moses in the bulrushes is neat enough to perform that service, and the showy leaves are not the only highlight of this package. The cradle-like bracts nestle into the foliage (the bulrushes, if you will) with their little blossoms. It's very cute.

One reason inch plants are so adored is that they grow in low light. I haven't pushed it; I usually give them a fairly bright east- or west-facing window. But I suspect you could sit them in a badly lit exposure and still make out fine. They might get a little stretchy, but pruning would help keep them looking smart. And don't feel apologetic about harboring these relics from the hippie era. Be green and be proud.

ZZ PLANT

To keep a ZZ plant from slipping into the shadows, give it a highly architectural role in your room.

Maybe you're an average Jane or John Doe living in a happy home with not-so-great light, and you have a corner to fill. You don't need flowers, and you prefer to keep the excitement confined to the television and computer screens. But you want something green in your life. Turn to the ZZ plant. You'll get a great plant that looks wonderful without any stress or strain on your busy schedule. I ignored ZZ until it walked into my life, and after that it was sort of like a Great Dane—big, sleek, affable, and easy.

I love that *Zamioculcas zamiifolia* takes up a generous chunk of real estate but doesn't require an equally dedicated allotment of time. The initial cash investment for a good-looking ZZ plant can be a little stiff. But obtain something sizable and well balanced from the get-go, as this plant can be sluggish when adding new growth. You get a series of swollen, almost palm-like stems that shoot from the base and are lined with shiny, waxy dark green leaves. Neatniks will love the shiny aspect because it looks like you pay someone to buff the plant daily, but no such elbow grease need be expended. ZZ plants are always dressed for success. I don't know why they aren't found in more public spaces.

The plant requires a generous footprint, but it also makes a statement from afar. A mature ZZ plant will be 36 inches (91 cm) tall but slender, so it's a nice vertical feature to play against your sofa and horizontal coffee tables. The trick lies in working with the plant to reach its potential. Start by giving it a container that will turn heads.

I tend to open my wallet for industrial-chic items, so I might be likely to plant ZZ in a metal cylinder. That works especially well for accommodating the roots and keeping this large plant from going thirsty. You could also drill holes in a sap bucket. I've also gone with concrete and given the plant a V-shaped nest surrounded by a cushion of selaginella moss. But you might want to take the opposite direction and enlist a sleek glazed terra-cotta container, especially if your living space is modern. The ZZ plant fits hand in glove with contemporary settings. If you go with glazed, you're playing off the plant's shiny leaves. If you select a matte finish, you'll complement the foliage, which might be an invitation to infuse bright colors into your decor. A container that pops ensures the ZZ plant doesn't just fade into the woodwork. The options are infinite.

You can bring this plant to the fore, but you don't have to give it more than a second thought in terms of maintenance. ZZ is the ultimate indestructible houseplant, no qualifications necessary.

Give it indirect light from an east- or west-facing window and water it when the soil is dry to your touch, and it will happily shine on. It won't grow by leaps and bounds, but it will add a few leaves now and then. The secret to a successful ZZ is acquiring a plant that looks fairly snazzy to begin with. The wait for wonderful might be prolonged if you go for something immature. Spring for a great looking plant and celebrate its glory.

And that is the message with all these indestructible houseplants. If you give them half a chance, they can be absolutely awesome. Each and every one of the plants in these pages can shine and make you proud, but will not steal a chunk of your time, attention, or resources. All you have to do is plug in your creativity and let it roll. This could change your life.

ZZ PLANT
Zamioculcas zamiifolia

EASIEST

SIZE	Ranging from 15 to 36 inches (38 to 91 cm) high
FOLIAGE	Fat, juicy stems lined with shiny, rounded leaves; very tidy
OTHER ATTRIBUTES	No flowers, but bulletproof
EXPOSURE	East or west
WATER REQUIREMENTS	Keep soil lightly moist but not soggy
OPTIMUM NIGHTTIME TEMPERATURE	50–80°F (10–27°C)
RATE OF GROWTH	Slow
SOIL TYPE	Good potting soil with compost included
FERTILIZING	Early spring to late autumn
ISSUES	Slow to form a good-looking plant
COMPANIONS	Ferns, ficus, mosses, prayer plants, rhipsalis, sansevierias, and tradescantia

THE
DETAILS

Previous spread:
Peperomias make
great adaptable
combo plants.

MAKING IT HAPPEN

Now that I've tantalized you with the options, here
are the nuts and bolts for making this happen in your
home, starting with selecting the right container and
moving into the specifics of display. The beauty of gardening indoors is that no matter where you live or
what type of style you favor, everything can be trans-
lated so it works for you.

SELECTING A GREEN ROOMMATE
Linking up with the right houseplant is a lot like finding someone compatible to share your life—except
houseplants don't have the same baggage, and if the
relationship doesn't work, moving along is so much
easier (at least theoretically). Thumb through these
pages, check out the photos, and select a plant that
appeals to you and fits with your growing situation.
Chemistry is everything.

My first piece of advice is similar to the one your
mother handed down when you started dating: Don't
necessarily settle for the first suitor that comes down
the pike. Wait for wonderful. Just because you have
less-than-ideal conditions doesn't mean you don't
deserve to find love. Indestructible plants can be cool.
Expect beauty or find the kinky green thing of your
dreams, but don't compromise.

Things might fall together perfectly, but let's zero in
on your specific set of conditions to improve your odds.
We've got plants here to handle all sorts of conditions
and situations. But the trick to success lies in focusing
on the appropriate playing field rather than groping
all over the plant kingdom and coming up with plants
that might not work for you.

Beyond the environment in your home, you might
also have personality traits that influence the best
plant choice. Chemistry is great, but you've got to be

Oh, the places you can go with your indestructible houseplants.
Philodendron cordatum 'Brasil' never looked so good.

practical too. We've all tried (and occasionally failed) to make the odd couple work. Rather than pushing your luck, think about who you are and choose accordingly.

If you tend to be a big-time nurturer who loves to water, steer clear of succulents. They hate soggy soil. Try going for a beefsteak plant (*Iresine*) instead. If you can't help but be overly generous with a container, avoid begonias, which prefer cramped roots. Instead, a Chinese evergreen (*Aglaonema*) or a fern would be a better bet. On the other hand, maybe you're so busy that you forget to water. A euphorbia, aspidistra, aloe, agave, or haworthia, or any of the succulents, won't hold a grudge.

At the same time, consider your growing conditions and personal style. Do plants that grope around give you the creepy-crawlies? Avoid hoyas, maidenhair vines, and ivies. Do you feel threatened by plants with thorns? Don't invite an agave into your life. Bored by plants that do nothing for protracted periods of time? Skip crotons and aspidistras.

Now for the positive column on your wish list. Want flowers? Try geraniums, flaming Katy, medinillas, or African violets. More interested in colorful foliage? A beefsteak plant (*Iresine*), prayer plant, or begonia would be a great fit. Like strong architectural statements? A bromeliad, aloe, or agave is just the ticket. Keen on the concept of a tree indoors? Adopt a Norfolk Island pine, false aralia, or mirror plant (*Coprosma*).

If you love to water, avoid succulent plants such as agaves.

CAUTIONS

This is a complex issue, but it's important to consider how plants interact with your family, especially children and pets. Many of the plants in this book are toxic. But toxicity is not a simple topic, and it requires more than a quick mention. I'm not an expert in the field. I keep it simple: *None of your houseplants should be eaten by people or pets*. Even plants that are not toxic might lead to an allergic reaction. Plus, plants might have been exposed to nonorganic pesticides before you acquired them. Plants can also have dermatological effects, and some sport thorns and barbs. Keep all plants out of reach of anyone or anything that might have a negative impasse with them, and always wear gloves when handling plants and potting soil. For more complete information on toxicity concerns, consult professionals before adopting a plant. Go to aspca.org/pet-care/poison-control/plants for information on issues with pets. For questions about human toxicity, call a physician and/or a poison control center, and refer to the American Association of Poison Control Centers at aapcc.org.

I often field questions about how I trained Einstein to cohabitate with my plants. I adopted him as a kitten from a local shelter. Initially I tried spraying plants with a cat deterrent before I introduced him to greenery. Then I let the little fellow interact with my menagerie, first ensuring no toxic plants were part of the experimental playing field. The oil spray I used had no effect whatsoever (and actually made him more curious), and it also ate holes in my orchid leaves. We had a few tough moments during Einstein's maiden explorations, but I gave him negative feedback whenever

Einstein admires a group of plants, but keeps his paws off them.

Alternanthera dentata 'Red Thread' basks in sunbeams. Although it would love a south-facing window, I can only provide a bright east-facing sill—and it works.

he seemed far too interested in a plant for the wrong motives. Any behavior that even slightly resembled nibbling elicited epic conniption fits. As a result (or perhaps for reasons that have nothing to do with my histrionics), Einstein does not ingest plants except the cat grass grown specifically for him. But to be on the safe side, I keep all plants that are particularly poisonous out of his reach, and I urge you to do likewise. I also tried to teach Einstein that ear-piercing screams and other frightening outbursts follow swiftly in the wake of plant mutilation, broken pots, and spilled soil. Unfortunately, he still occasionally launches himself before considering that what goes up must come down. Crash landings occur. We're working on it.

LIGHT

The light available in your home will come into play when you choose plants. A south-facing window tends to be the brightest exposure and does a great job of supporting sun-worshipping plants such as succulents. But most of the plants in this book don't demand a south window and will do fine in those that face east or west. Even zonal geraniums will perform beautifully and flower to beat the band in a bright east- or west-facing window. In winter, I find that west is brighter than east, so start there if you've got a zonal geranium, beefsteak plant, evolvulus, alternanthera, or any other plant you're trying to keep compact and/ or blooming. North-facing windows are the last resort, and might lead to heartache unless you're nurturing something like aspidistras, ferns, ivies, or moss.

Don't assume that plants want a sunbeam promotion. Begonias and African violets will burn in a south-facing window, and other plants have a similar reaction. Follow the particular recommendations for each plant. That said, every home is different. If a building stands between your window and the sun, it might obstruct the incoming light. Porch overhangs also tend to shade windows. On the flip side, if you live beside a body of water or have a pool close by, its reflection might increase the available light. Snow does a great job of augmenting the brightness index. Where you position a plant in a window can affect its ability to gather in the beams. Plants placed close to the windowpanes will enjoy prime light. The farther away you sit a plant, the less light is available. But many of the indestructibles can survive just fine within 36 inches (91 cm) of a window and sometimes farther; experiment to find out what works best. Fortunately, plants have a clever way of conveying when they need more lumens. When they bend toward the light source, that's your cue to move them closer and rotate their containers. (Rotating is a good practice in all circumstances. It's your best shot at getting balanced light in a window.) Light coming from more than one angle (like a bay window or a corner position) is optimal. Keep in mind that tall and/or broad plants close to the window will cut off incoming light for their neighbors, when staging plants strategically according to their light needs. Window treatments also stand in the way of light and your plants. I go with sheer.

HUMIDITY

Humidity can be a stumbling block for many potential indoor gardeners. None of the plants in this book demands high humidity. However, if your house is so dry that your skin feels like a lizard's and your cat is sparking, you might consider increasing the humidity for everyone's comfort. Certain types of heat tend to steal moisture from the air. Wood-burning stoves and forced hot air are notorious culprits. But there are solutions.

Humidifiers are a great way to increase atmospheric humidity in a home. Another solution is a pebble tray.

A pebble tray is an effective means of increasing humidity immediately around plants.

Fill a tray (even a roasting pan will do) with 1 inch (2.5 cm) of pebbles and pour ½ inch (1 cm) of water on the bottom. Be sure to keep it filled as it evaporates around the plants. Another idea is to grow your plants in the bathroom, which tends to be more humid than the rest of the house, especially if you take frequent showers. If your bathroom furnishes sufficient light, give it a try.

The more plants you grow, the more humidity they create for their companions, including you. When I deliver water to my plants, especially in winter when all the windows are closed, I can feel my sinuses opening up. All that damp soil works its magic.

A commonly attempted—and ineffective—method for raising humidity is misting. This only momentarily increases the moisture in the air immediately around a plant. It's wasted effort. You would have to apply mist every few minutes around the clock to make an impact.

TEMPERATURES

I live chilly. My house is downright cold. If I'm not wearing a heavy sweater in winter, I'm uncomfortable. In a converted barn it's pretty much impossible to get the temperature above 60°F (15°C). Usually it hovers around 58°F (14°C) during the day and 53°F (12°C) at night (nighttime temperatures are the low point of the range in each listing). My home environment isn't typical, but the plants survive beautifully—even the begonias. I do have trouble with certain plants. I cannot grow streptocarpus (aka Cape primroses) and several other members of the African violet group, even though I would love to do so. They simply prefer a warmer climate. I've mentioned this problem in the African violet section, and offered alternatives.

On the flip side, your living space might be toasty. In a very warm home, the heat tends to suck humidity out of the air. Temperatures of 80°F (27°C) or above will cause frequent wilting. Even worse, insects just love lounging around in high temperatures. How about striving for a happy medium?

People often ask about the dangers of keeping plants too close to cold windowpanes. It's usually not an issue with insulated glass or storm windows. But if you feel that your plant is suffering from the chill, pull it away from the panes.

FINDING A CONTAINER

Now comes the really fun part: matching the plant and container. I often find a great vessel and then shop for a plant to match. But there is more to consider than aesthetics. Although indestructibles are flexible, your job will be so much easier if you give a plant the root room it needs. On the other hand, you don't want the plant to swim. Choose a container that is at least 2 to 3 inches (5 to 7 cm) larger than the diameter of the pot in which the plant currently dwells.

Everyone has heard the expression about how uncomfortably round pegs sit in square holes. With plants, it's not an issue because the root systems are pliable. Feel free to pot a round root system in a square receptacle and vice versa, but take care to fill in the spaces. Be sure to find a container that is slightly deeper than the original, even though you'll rough up the roots slightly when transplanting.

Unless I've purchased a plant in a glam container (which almost never happens), I repot immediately when I adopt. In fact, few plants reside in my sight for twenty-four hours before receiving a makeover. Generally houseplants come into the fold with pitiful plastic containers in decidedly yuck colors. I make haste to remedy that situation. Sometimes I have a container in mind the moment I see the plant. In other cases I go shopping.

You can find containers that are incredibly diverse. There is no need to go with standard fare.

Footed urns, like this one cradling pilea and moss, drain more rapidly than other containers. If you tend to forget to water, go a different route when selecting a pot.

Most container shapes work admirably for houseplants. You can't go wrong with the standard cone shape. When a container has a gradual flare going from its base to a wider mouth, it performs its function brilliantly. Water is delivered evenly throughout, and you can easily extract that plant for graduations. On the other hand, a bean jar shape with a mouth that tapers in from a broader midrib can be a major stumbling block for repotting. Even worse is a container with a broad footprint and a much smaller mouth. Don't do that to yourself.

Footed and pedestal containers tend to drain quickly. If you are not able to water frequently, avoid that shape. It's a pity, because they are enticingly handsome. But let practicality rule. However, if you're growing a plant that dotes on great drainage, such as a succulent, this can work in your favor.

Clay is the standard for houseplant pots, and you can't go wrong with a simple clay pot. Hand-thrown terra-cotta is even snazzier, and glazed terra-cotta also works beautifully. But that's just the tip of the iceberg. You can also work with zinc, cement, metal, or anything else that looks fantastic. Find a look that's in sync with your decor.

I often turn to alternative containers instead of typical pots. I use anything from buckets to umbrella stands to house my houseplants, and many of these repurposed artifacts require drainage holes. I don't drill anything that's very valuable, but most things in my life are rummage. My drill buddy uses a masonry drill bit for clay and a metal drill bit for any other type of container. The small drill bits are less likely to damage a container.

Don't assume that containers purchased specifically for plants will have drainage. Nowadays many containers do not have holes, so you'll have to drill them. Always check, because some pots are fitted with

If a container isn't too valuable, drill holes, especially when you're repurposing something that wasn't originally intended to serve as a plant pot. More than one hole is necessary to effectively drain the soil.

Ingredients for potting a container without drainage.

Pouring the pebbles into the container.

pinhole-size drainage, which isn't effective. On the flip side, some pots have massive holes that allow too much soil to escape. When faced with this situation, I cut up the mesh bags that bulbs (like tulips) arrive in and insert little squares over the holes on the inside of the pot. You can also use pot shards as crocking over a hole. I have found that orchid pots are not particularly practical, even for orchids. Not only does the potting

medium escape through the oversize holes, but water spills out all over. Any terra-cotta container with ample drainage works fine for orchids if you grow them in an appropriate medium.

In my constant quest to be kinky, I have occasionally used oddball containers like colanders. They are great for growing succulents that love generous drainage (couple them with a plant that can withstand

Mixing horticultural charcoal with the pebbles.

Adding soil and plants.

drought). But keep in mind that they will leak from the sides. I situate them on trays and clean up the spills afterward. Another solution is to line the sides with plastic and leave the bottom to drain naturally.

I love using old enamelware for houseplants, and you can get it for a song, especially if it's chipped. If you don't want to drill, line the bottom of the container with a shallow layer of ⅜ inch gravel mixed with

a tablespoon of horticultural charcoal (available at most nurseries, but you can also find it at aquarium supply stores). This method works for any pot that doesn't have drainage. The charcoal acts like a filter and prevents any extra water from going stagnant and smelling like a bog. Pour the pebbles into the bottom of the container, add the charcoal, and mix it together with the pebbles as your bottom layer. Then add potting soil, dig holes, and plant directly in the soil. No need to worry if the pebble-charcoal layer mixes with the potting soil while you're in the process of potting.

The balancing act with containers is to find something you love that is also functional. Remember that any living thing can be compromised. The container you select can spell the difference between high maintenance and a piece of cake.

FINDING A SAUCER

Saucers are imperative. If you don't have a method for keeping water from dribbling out of the drainage holes and spilling all over, you are going to make a mess.

Although I have no fine furniture in my life, I'm fond of my decor and don't want it to be ruined. Matching plants with their underpinnings is a design challenge that I enjoy immensely. When all my plants come in from their summer sojourn to bask indoors, I delight in matching them up with my various saucers. The best ones are glazed inside and out. Plain terra-cotta can stain furniture. In fact, any saucer laid directly on a surface has the potential for leaving a mildew stain. You might consider laying a round piece of cork beneath it (you can buy them specifically for plants,

precut to the right size). Another solution is to use a zinc tray with a lip to serve as a substitute for saucers. I often take this route because it looks great with my industrial retro home. Putting a placemat underneath a saucer also works well.

Saucers should be slightly wider than the containers they are serving. A saucer that is too small is useless for its purpose. Actually, it's worse than impractical: It can give you a false sense of security and you might forget to check for spills, which can ruin furniture, carpeting, and flooring, and can also be a safety issue. On the other hand, if a saucer is too large, sitting water can cause problems. If your pet is in the bad habit of accessing water from saucers, empty them immediately. If your plant is hard to lift, use a turkey baster to eliminate excess water.

For every quandary you might face when establishing houseplants into your home and making them comfortable, there are plenty of solutions. If I didn't think that you could do this beautifully, I wouldn't be nudging you in the green direction. But if you approach a plant as a potential work of art and position yourself as the artist, even the saucer it sits on is raised to another level of importance.

There is no need to be confined to saucers sold at a nursery. You can enlist plates and tins as well.

Adding some vintage glass insulators to your aloe planter raises the level of savvy several degrees.

Multiples of selaginella mosses make a sharp scene. Just one wouldn't convey the same expressive statement.

A false aralia mini forest with a pilea ground cover and stones feels like a scene from outside.

MIXING AND MATCHING

Of course you want more than one plant in your company. You want plenty. You crave a garden inside. The beauty of indestructibles is that the individual players will not be high maintenance, so you can have indoor greenery without rearranging your social calendar. These diehards will not take up a big chunk of time, but they might change the way you live in your home.

With lots of plants nearby, you might spend more time in-house. Rather than wandering off to find nature, you can locate it inside. That's part of the beauty of growing plants indoors. Host a group of aralias or Norfolk Island pines and, bingo, you've got a forest. Of course, don't skimp on the hiking. But when you've just dragged yourself home from the office, you can have an exhale moment right in the comfort of your kitchen.

Sometimes making that scene requires multiples. Lining up a group of the same plant, each echoing its neighbors is extremely articulate. In other cases, you might want to combine ferns with mosses and maybe even a rock or two. It's a lot like landscaping in miniature. Create a scene that lowers your blood pressure and gives you that sigh of relief you previously found only outdoors. Find a way to incorporate it into your house. This might require recruiting some furniture into another purpose. You also might need some trays; I enlist a lot of zinc and metal baking sheets, which serve all sorts of functions, including catching drips and acting as a base. Those with a lip are particularly useful.

MAKING MATCHES

Indestructible plants combine easily, and that's where you can really exercise your creative yin-yang. You can pull together a great little garden on the inside of your windows, complete with all the elements you hold dear outdoors. Nestle together textures that have a meaningful dialogue. Play off the hues in your decor by matching or complementing the upholstery, curtains, painted furniture, wall colors, wallpaper, art pieces, or accessories. But you can also combine leaf or flower colors and profile them to their best advantage. Consider the container too. Make sure your playmates are compatible.

Use the companion suggestions in the Gallery of Indestructibles to guide your selections of diehards that might sit side by side. If you suspect certain plants would make a great combination, give it a try. When plants are potted separately, it's easy enough to reshuffle if something isn't working out. You can also rearrange elements as they come in and out of flower. You can play favorites together when they're prime. There's no end to the fun you can have working with easy houseplants in your home.

MIXED CONTAINERS

You can also drop jaws, raise eyebrows, and flex your creative muscles by growing indestructibles together in the same container. The result is stupendous. It moves houseplants into a whole different arena that is more like garden design in miniature. You don't need real estate. Anybody can do it. Suddenly you have all the benefits of an outdoor garden throughout the year in the comfort of your home.

When you combine plants of the same genus—like growing peperomias in the same container as other peperomias or ferns with ferns—the guesswork is simpler. The selection process is streamlined when you're

Going with only peperomias is an easy way to match cultural requirements.

looking at just one family, and you stand the best chance of finding plants that enjoy the same cultural requirements. But think about the aesthetics of color combinations, height and size complements, and the textural conversation. Just like planting a garden, consider using plants that are upright beside plants that sprawl while playing different textures together. Most important, select a balanced group of plants that won't be weighted by one larger team player working in a tug-of-war against a slew of smaller compatriots. Check the mature size of individuals before pulling together your mini scene. You don't want any rude surprises later in the game.

Be practical when you create your composition.

Try potting ferns together in a combination planter

Be sure to water a mutual container after potting.

Select a container that is sufficiently broad to entertain all the plants that are invited to the party; after all, they might be living together for a while. Give them all they need to make the relationship harmonious. The container might be round (I often harness enamel bowls for the purpose), rectangular (such as a vintage wooden file drawer), or shaped like a window box. Be sure to match the planting container with a saucer, baking sheet, or pan to catch the inevitable drips.

The easiest way to create a mixed container that needs only easy upkeep is to find a vessel with a drainage hole or holes (or you can drill the holes yourself). If the container has no drainage, line the bottom of the pot with a 1-inch (2.5 cm) layer of ⅜ inch pebbles mixed with charcoal (see Making It Happen, page 250). Fill the container with potting soil. Select the plants that you want to use as fillers, keeping design principles in mind. Remove them from their pots and loosen roots that are tightly wound in the previous container. Dig the first receiving hole in the container and repeat for each plant that you tuck in. Insert the plants evenly throughout the container and be sure to add sufficient soil around their edges so that no empty holes remain around each plant. A pencil or a kebab with a cork fitted on one end can help press soil into the tight spaces between plants. Firm the plants into the soil carefully, which will mean the difference between success and failure in the planter. Water the container and position it near a light source. Monitor it and water when needed while the plants are acclimating to communal life. The end result can be exhilarating, meaningful, and fulfilling.

EDGING-PLANT COMBINATIONS

Making combination planters is a great indoor sport, but it's not the only avenue for working plants into a mutual dialogue in the same container. Try using plants as edging to cover the soil around an upright plant or to dangle below a taller compatriot. If you have an aglaonema that stands upright, try planting moss and pilea around its ankles. They all enjoy similar growing conditions, and they make a great package. You will achieve a masterpiece worthy of turning heads and provoking envy without creating additional work for yourself.

ADDING NATURE AND FAVORITE THINGS

Houseplants are a great way to bring the outdoors into your living space, but don't stop there. Add the beauty of nature into your scene by using all the little treasures you tucked into your pockets on your hikes and walks. They can find an expressive place to dwell together with plants. Whether it's seashells from a summer spent beachcombing or arrowheads from the desert, you can combine them with your plants to create a dialogue. A lichen-covered stick, a pinecone, or a rock with a pleasing shape can make your planting shine. You can insert them into the picture with individual plants, using prunings from your trees and shrubs instead of trellises, perhaps, or putting a fossil into the base of any pot. Or you can add sweetgum balls or other seedpods, or anything else you've brought home from outdoors, as part of the artwork in a combination planter. When you pull together a group of indestructible plants, remember that it's all about you. Whatever you create has the potential to say the world about who you are inside and what you value. Let the story take shape.

Aglaonema 'Queen of Siam' shoots upright from the container, so filling around it with *Selaginella kraussiana* 'Aurea' and *Pilea grandis* 'Aquamarine' makes a stronger visual statement.

Add nature such as pinecones, *abandoned* honeycomb (be sure it's no longer in use!), and birch bark to the scene.

With a stern haircut this plecthranthus looks like a runway model.

INDESTRUCTIBLE BASICS

Nothing living is totally hands-off, and no plant is completely indestructible. Although the plants in this book are comparatively low maintenance, they do need some care. Giving them love also helps. They will tolerate some abuses, but be kind. The better you treat them, the more beautiful they will become. These plants are easy, and they easily make your life gorgeous. But don't completely forget them. Here's how you can make their lives happy while making your life green.

WATERING

Watering is the chore that is most often forgotten. We've all occasionally skipped a visit with the watering can. The plants in this book can tolerate an occasional lapse. Whether they survive multiple transgressions has a lot to do with the time of year, the brightness of light, the weather, the indoor environment, and how often you neglect the drinks. But try not to put them to the test.

When I lecture, audience members sit with their pens poised, hoping I will advise them to water every Tuesday or the like. It doesn't work that way. Few things in nature are linked with our calendars. Watering has more to do with the weather and the environment, and these factors are continually changing. One week the weather might be sunny and hot and your houseplants will dry out often. You might need to water every other day. Another week will be drizzly and chilly. You might need to water only once, and your succulents will not require any water whatsoever. Then again, it might be miserably cold outdoors. Even though the sun isn't shining brightly, your furnace is running nonstop. That heat can dry out plants, and they will need more drinks.

Use the sensitivity method. Most indestructible plants prefer water when their soil is dry to the touch. Allowing them to go parched will lead to problems. How do you know when they're too dry? Wilted or shriveled leaves are a dead giveaway. Many of the plants in this book will spring back from a serious wilt, but if you keep inflicting this sort of cruel treatment, they will fall victim to pest and disease problems. Don't get that started. Instead, be attentive.

Proper watering is a learned skill. Test the soil with your finger by inserting it into the soil and feeling for moisture. You can also try the pencil trick: Stick the eraser end of a pencil into the soil and withdraw it. If the pencil comes out clean, the soil is probably dry. If a little wet soil adheres to the eraser head, there's moisture in the soil. Or you can look at the soil color—dry soil is a shade paler than moist soil. Or lift the plant up and feel its weight. Moist soil is heavier than dry soil. Apply water before heroic measures are necessary. When soil becomes too dry, it fails to sponge up water properly. That's when water runs down the sides of the soil and straight out the drainage hole without moistening the medium. In that case, submerge the pot in a saucer of water and let it take up the moisture gradually from below. After that stopgap measure, you should be able to water normally again.

How much water should you apply? Ideally, you should have an empty ½ inch (1 cm) or more of space between the soil line and the rim of the pot. Fill that reservoir with water and let it slowly quench the soil. You should only need to fill the reservoir once per application. Let the plant slurp up the water and then wait to visit it again when it's ready for another drink.

Make watering as easy as possible by using a watering can with a small spout that you can easily point at the target.

FERTILIZING

People love to feed things, and plants respond to a healthy diet. I take the organic approach and furnish my plants with a potting soil that is enriched with loam and compost. It's not a soilless mix. When I newly repot a plant (see the following section), it has access to a lot of oomph. I usually wait a few months after repotting before I apply additional fertilizer.

I fertilize once every three to four weeks with an organic fertilizer. Most brands use some sort of fish emulsion to deliver the goods to the plant's roots. Always dilute the fertilizer according to the label recommendations, and water it into the soil as you would normally water the plant. Expect to smell something fishy. The label claims that there is no odor, but let's get real. Plan your fertilizing gig to occur right before you go on a shopping spree, then leave for a few hours. When you return, the smell has usually dissipated.

I generally don't fertilize between late autumn and early spring because light levels are lower and houseplants do not need anything extra—most of them are slipping into their slow mode. If a plant appears to be pale, give it some food. But most of the plants in this book are not gluttonous types. On my last feeding in autumn and my first feeding in spring it's always wise to taper off and build up to feeding gradually. I dilute the fertilizer to half-strength to allow the plants to become accustomed to the new regimen.

REPOTTING

Plants that have filled their containers with roots and are ready to be graduated tend to drink heavily and become maintenance issues. Even the most amiable plant can become a burden when it's pot-bound (that is, when the roots have filled the container and are ready for a graduation). If a plant wilts often, that's one indication it might need a larger container. Look

Healthy roots ready for repotting.

for a network of plump, healthy roots wrapping around the soil. If half the soil is not visible, it's time for a promotion.

Selecting the right soil is key to a healthy plant. Going organic is a great choice. I don't mix my own potting soil. There are plenty of good packaged soils available (see the Sources section) at garden centers, and mixing my own would entail sterilizing soils and the like. Don't bother. A good potting soil has ample drainage and good texture, and it does not become muddy when you water. Testing the proper consistency is easy. Just moisten the soil, clench it into a loose fist, and open your fist. If the soil crumbles apart, that's

Soil that is best suited for growing plants will crumble after you squeeze it in your fist.

good. If it remains in one soggy glob, that's not good.

When repotting, put a little bed of good soil into the new container. Before inserting the plant, tease out the roots from the root ball so they aren't wrapped tightly around in the shape of the former container. Position the plant so the top of the root ball is ½ to 1 inch (1 to 2 cm) below the rim of the pot. Fill in the sides with soil. This is the tricky part. If any air pockets remain, the roots will dry out, so be sure to pack it. You don't want to cement the soil in, but use your finger or a pencil to fill all the spaces. Tap the newly repotted plant against the repotting table a few times to settle the soil down and fill in any soft edges. Water the newly repotted plant fully. It should be good to go for many months in its new home.

Loosen the root ball and tease the roots free so the previous pot's imprint isn't so distinct.

Fill the soil around the root ball.

One quick word of caution: Don't repot a plant when it appears to be suffering from disease. Giving it a promotion rarely solves the problem and usually leads to more issues. And don't assume you can skip a few steps by giving a plant a huge container. If roots have too much room and cannot slurp up excess moisture, the soil tends to stay damp, and that's not good. Don't move it up more than 2 to 3 inches (5 to 7 cm) at a time.

Firm the soil around the root ball of the plant.

Water your plant in its new home.

PROPAGATION

A grisly crash echoes through the house, followed by the scampering of little paws making a speedy getaway. When I get to the scene of the crime, Einstein is nowhere to be found (surprise, surprise), but the rhizomatous begonia he left in his wake is a wreck. Even worse, its Guy Wolff container is now pot shards. The terra-cotta is history. But the begonia is salvageable, and now I have a stimulus package to propagate a bunch of leaf wedges to share with friends.

Not all diehard plants are easy to propagate, but many do streamline the sharing process. In the case of the rhizomatous begonia, I just need to cut the leaf into wedges, starting at the middle, so each wedge has a little bit of the central sinus. Then I dip the wedge in rooting hormone, push one third of the wedge into sharp sand (you could also use potting soil, but make sure to let it dry out slightly between moistenings), and put it under a cloche. In a couple of months, I'm raising a family. Or, if (and when) Einstein manages to break off a little aboveground rhizome on the begonia, I can tuck that into another pot and have extras. Not only is it a way to smooth over a pet's antics, but rooting cuttings can also be an outlet when you've pruned.

Leaf wedges are not the easiest way to propagate a plant, and this method does not work for most plants. Many houseplants are more simply reproduced from stem cuttings. Among the easiest are beefsteak plants (*Iresine*), geraniums, hoyas, ivies, kalanchoes, peperomias, philodendrons, pileas, polka dot plants, rhipsalis, senecios, spider plants, and tradescantias. In some cases you don't even need rooting hormone to work your magic (although it always speeds the process along). Just nip off the top 2 to 3 inches (5 to 7 cm) of a healthy stem (select growth that isn't very young and tender or very old and woody) and tuck it into potting soil. Keep the soil moderately moist (but not soggy) while roots are initiating. High humidity will prevent the foliage from wilting, but you might want to cut off large leaves or snip them in half. In most cases a cloche helps out, but it isn't a deal-breaker.

You can also divide up other plants. I don't know why people shy away from this task. If you do it carefully, you'll have multiple plants. Of course, the footprint of the mother plant will be diminished temporarily, but it usually bulks up again in no time. Easily divided plants include agaves (watch out for those thorns!), aloes, bromeliads, carex, hens and chicks, mosses, prayer plants, sansevierias, and silver squill. Before you divide, make sure the pups have roots. If

Even while they're rooting, iresine cuttings look intriguing underneath a cloche. There's no reason you can't make the process visually appealing.

not, treat them like cuttings and give them the moist-soil-and-high-humidity treatment. If they have roots, simply pot each section into its own container (which is usually smaller than the original home), water it as if you were repotting, and put it in a shady spot for a week or so while it recuperates from the shuffle.

PRUNING

Don't fear pruning. In most cases, the outcome is excellent. You do a little nipping and tucking, and you

This schefflera was already pruned once, and you can see it's on the way to being beautiful. But a gawky stem remains.

Give that long, spindly stem a snip where you want it to branch out.

come out with a plant that has a new lease on life. It feels proud, it branches out, it makes you beam. It's worth the risk.

Most gardeners leave pruning until the eleventh hour or later, and it becomes a stopgap measure before ditching the plant because it's gone from ravishing to ragged. Don't do that. Brandish the shears early in the game, before it is emergency surgery. Clipping stems encourages them to branch, leading to a broader, fuller end result. If you break into a cold sweat

at the idea, pinch the emerging bud from the tip of a stem. You won't even see the cosmetic procedure, but the plant will branch and the end result will be the same.

The effectiveness of pruning has a lot to do with when you've gathered the gumption to make the move. The earlier, the better. If you finally take action when the plant has become spindly, it might be necessary to make a deep cut lower on the stem, which leads to a temporarily gawky plant. Don't assume a

This trailing plectranthus is getting shaggy. Time for a haircut.

It seems drastic, but the end result will be fabulous. Trust me.

The nearly shorn plectranthus.

plant will branch all the way up and down the stem when you clip the tip. Often it branches only below the place where you've beheaded it.

Watch out for so-called blind eyes. Some plants, like zonal geraniums and begonias, put tremendous energy into producing flower stalks and skip the impulse to branch, so there are no shoots at intervals where the leaves jut out. Look for a side branch before you make a cut, but don't sweat it if you forget. The worst thing that can happen is you'll have a naked stem that you can later clip, but no branching. Many plants also sprout from the base when you snip their growing tips, so you get even more expansion for your efforts.

GROOMING

This task is easy and obvious, but we all neglect to do it. Even indestructible plants will have unsightly leaves every once in a while. Whisk them away. Brown or disfigured leaves are not going to improve. Similarly, pull a plant away from its neighbors every once in a while and check out all its body parts. If some aspect is not improving its overall appearance, clip it or clean it up. Remember that you're in charge of the dress code.

PESTS

People worry a lot about pests, and these concerns are understandable. I have hundreds of plants in my domain, but I am very rarely pestered by pests. I have no real issues because I grow organically, I water regularly, I heed a plant's light preferences, and I steer away from plants that are bug magnets. In other words, I grow indestructibles.

Healthy plants tend to avoid becoming victims. When plants are stressed, insects attack the weakened target—and almost always win. This book recommends plants that are unlikely to easily succumb to stress. But evil things can happen.

First and foremost, check plants before you bring them home. Examine the undersides of leaves, and look closely for wildlife. Don't assume that a nursery has you covered. Bring your reading glasses when you go looking for plants—if you want, bring a magnifier. Don't feel apologetic about turning a plant upside down and examining its root system. I find that hens and chicks are prone to root mealybug, and I don't think twice about checking their roots. If someone has a problem with it, I take my business elsewhere.

When I bring a plant home, I keep it segregated from other plants for a week or so while I assess its health and well-being. Any reputable nursery should be willing to take a plant back and/or refund your money if you find evidence of pests or diseases immediately after purchase (assuming you haven't waited several weeks or treated it roughly in the meantime). But take steps to make sure you don't infest the rest of your healthy plants with problems from newbies.

Another line of defense I practice is to grow my plants in cool temperatures. Actually, I do this during

That brown leaf on *Pelargonium* 'A Happy Thought' needs to go.

winter because it's difficult to heat a converted barn, but being economical works in my favor because insects prefer dry, toasty conditions. On the rare occasions when I have an insect attack, it usually occurs in early spring, when the temperatures warm up to nurture opportunistic bugs.

We live in an imperfect world. You might be a novice, or your plants could come to you with issues. The best strategy is to become educated about problems and have a battle strategy in place.

Always read the label before using an insecticide, even if it is an organic product. Read, understand, and follow the manufacturer's recommendations and precautions. I always spray or treat a plant outdoors and let the spray dry before I bring the plant back into the fold, no matter how benign an organic product might seem. Always wear gloves, long sleeves, and protective clothing and eye gear. Keep insecticides (even organic solutions) away from pets and children. Always make sure a product is designed to address the issue that you're trying to combat.

Your list of pests might vary depending on where you live, but these are usual suspects. Aphids are the most frequent pest for indoor plants. They can appear suddenly and increase rapidly. Aphids are rarely found as single attackers; they usually strike as an army. They tend to cluster on new growth, and they are about the size of an ant or smaller, but they have soft bodies. When you see them, they have usually attained population-explosion numbers. Fortunately, they also succumb to most organic soap-based plant sprays. Beyond aphids, common houseplant critters include spider mites. These tiny red insects form webs, usually on the underside of a plant, although large colonies will weave webs elsewhere. You can usually dispatch them with a cold stream of water—they hate cold, wet conditions. Mealybugs, which form tiny cotton-like wads on stems and leaves, are another common foe. They are difficult to treat, and I usually end up sending the affected plant to the compost pile. Root mealybugs, which form cottony masses in a plant's root system, are a bear. I forfeit the plant instead of trying to fight them. Whitefly (when you jostle the plant, a cloud of white, flying insects dart around) can be caught with sticky traps. Scale, which looks like a brown bump on the stem or leaf, is a problem you can fight with horticultural oils, but ferns tend to be sensitive, so avoid spraying them. Fungus gnats are unsightly, but they are not a health issue for your plants. When the soil of plants is kept continually moist and not allowed to dry out between waterings, fungus gnats have a ball. If you change the plant's environment, the problem should disappear. When in doubt about the identity of a pest or a remedy, contact your state agricultural extension station. Staff members are trained to help you.

In addition to these methods, there are all sorts of organic remedies at your disposal. Those should be your first go-to solutions before you bring out the big guns. I prefer to toss a plant rather than fiddle with toxic sprays, especially for a plant that dwells in my home. I urge you to adopt the same position.

DISEASES

Cleanliness is the best tactic for keeping plants healthy. Although I've selected plants that are not prone to problems, you never know. To keep your little kingdom free of blight, remove any leaf that has the slightest hint of an issue. Be suspicious of holes on leaves or marred foliage. Don't wait for a leaf to dissolve before taking action. Any malady left unchecked is likely to spread.

However, removing a leaf might not be the end of your trouble. Issues in the environment cause most disease problems. Maybe you're keeping a succulent too moist when it prefers a dry atmosphere. Perhaps you're wetting the leaves of your African violet, which dislikes wet foliage. Take a moment to check the cultural requirements of the plant you are hosting and make sure you are on the right track. Keep in mind that all plants—except perhaps aquatic plants (and they are not prevalent in these pages)—detest stagnant soil that isn't draining. That's an invitation for disease issues to strike.

Think about how to correct the situation. Maybe you should water more or less often, or give the plant more or less light. As with pests, diseases generally result from stress. Don't pour on the fertilizer or give a pot promotion when a plant is ill. You wouldn't force a feast on someone in the hospital. Do give your plant a checkup. Explore the root system to make sure it's healthy. If you find brown roots rather than plump healthy versions, the plant might need to be downsized and potted into a tighter container. You might have to play Sherlock Holmes to get answers. Again, a great resource is your state agricultural extension station. I hope this won't be necessary. After all, you are growing indestructibles. They can grin their way through a lot.

Like many people, Lee Link often picks up zonal geraniums that strike her fancy but are not labeled. They are wonderful midwinter bloomers nonetheless.

HOUSEPLANT CALENDAR

Gardening is all about syncopation. Although you should not be a slave to a watering schedule, it's helpful to think about what you should do and when to do it. Unlike your garden outdoors, the pattern isn't always obvious, even though seasonal cues indirectly drive your indoor gardening schedule. Here are some brief ideas for care points to address at the right moment, starting with autumn, when houseplant season begins.

AUTUMN
No doubt you've brought houseplants outside to romp on patios or decks. Take them back indoors gradually, before frost makes seeking shelter imperative. Acclimate them to the conditions before your furnace starts blasting.

Check for insects.

If possible, stage plants in their permanent winter locations with saucers.

Do not place plants directly in front of or near heat vents.

In most cases, cease fertilizing in late autumn and withhold fertilizer throughout the winter.

Keep in mind that your watering schedule might be slightly reduced to address lower light and shorter days.

Unless a plant has increased dramatically, don't repot in autumn. Give promotions in spring.

Prune plants that have become overly large due to summer growth.

WINTER
Monitor for watering carefully; although light levels might not be bright, the furnace can dry out plants.

Move sun-loving plants closer to the panes (but not directly touching the glass).

Rotate plants so every angle enjoys light.
Prune back leggy growth caused by lower light; this will encourage branching.

SPRING

Don't rush to bring plants outdoors when the weather is still unstable. Instead, open windows.

Ventilation is key, so crack open those windows to keep insect problems at bay.

Repot any plants that need a graduation, but promote only one pot size at a time.

Begin fertilizing in early spring, but go with an increased dilution (more water, less fertilizer) for the first feedings. Then follow the dilution recommendations on the label.

When you're getting spring showers, watering might not be needed for several days. When the weather is warm and sunny, monitor for watering needs.

SUMMER

Bring plants outdoors for a summer sojourn, but take care not to put shade-loving plants in sunny locations. Even sun-worshippers will burn if transitioned from a window indoors to a seemingly equally bright location outside. It's safest to bring plants out when the weather will be cloudy for a few days, or to cover the plants temporarily.

Position outdoor plants away from windy locations, especially if they are large or have plus-size leaves. Be sure to give plants sufficient ballast so they don't blow over. Tall, thin pots are particularly prone to being toppled.

Be aware of roof runoff areas, and don't position plants in their direct line of drip. If possible, put succulents in a protected location covered by an overhang so

In summer, Marianne Vandenburgh moves most of her houseplants onto screened porches, including heart-leaf ivy, *Hedera helix* 'Ovata'.

they don't get drenched in storms.

Don't forget to water your plants. They can dry out rapidly outside.

Leave a few plants inside. You need something indoors during summer. Although you might be dividing your time between garden chores, the low-maintenance plants in this book won't need a whole lot of hand-holding.

FINALE

Think about what plants can do to improve your life. Consider how your home will feel when you walk in and see green stationed all around. Imagine waking up to a houseplant or maybe five little green guys sitting in the window not far from your bed. Even if you thought this was not within your realm, even if you have no time and seemingly no talent for growing houseplants, this book should change your mind.

When I wrote *The Unexpected Houseplant* a few years ago, I realized that lots of you want to live intimately with plants. You love the look and you long to cohabitate with plant life on an intimate basis. But you're not ready for a challenge. You want to wade in slowly and test out your windows with plants that will survive imperfection. This book is for you.

I hope you now feel enabled. My goal in writing this book is never again to hear the words *brown thumb* in association with houseplants. Everybody can grow them. Plus, there's no reason why you shouldn't have knock-'em-dead-gorgeous green works of art living close by. You just need to wander through these pages and draw up a wish list. There's something here for everyone. This will be the beginning of green and you. Think it cannot happen in your home? Think again. With indestructible houseplants, anything is possible.

Using faux wood stumps from Pergola, David Whitman tucked in *Peperomia rotundifolia*, *P. ferreyrae*, and an unidentified peperomia species.

SOURCES

PLANTS

Ballek's Garden Center
90 Maple Ave.
East Haddam, CT 06423
balleksgardencenter.com

Cortina Gardens
25 Bridgewater Rd.
New Milford, CT 06776

Dietrich Gardens
155 Main St. N
Woodbury, CT 06798
dietrichgardens.com

Glasshouse Works
Stewart, OH 45778
glasshouseworks.com

Goldner Walsh Nursery
559 Orchard Lake Rd.
Pontiac, MI 48341
goldnerwalsh.com

Hollandia Nurseries
95 Stony Hill Rd.
Bethel, CT 06801
ctgrown.com

Lauray of Salisbury
432 Undermountain Rd.
Salisbury, CT 06068
lauray.com

Logee's Greenhouses
141 North St.
Danielson, CT 06239
logees.com

Peckham's Greenhouse
200 West Main Rd.
Little Compton, RI 02837
peckhamsgreenhouse.com

Pergola
7 E. Shore Rd.
New Preston, CT 06777
pergolahome.com

Shakespeare's Garden
25 Obtuse Rd. S
Brookfield, CT 06804
shakespearesgarden.net

Snug Harbor Farm
87 Western Ave.
Kennebunk, ME 04043
snugharborfarm.com

Terrain at Styer's
914 Baltimore Pike
Glen Mills, PA 19342
shopterrain.com

CONTAINERS

Ben Wolff Pottery
305 Litchfield Tpk.
New Preston, CT 06777
benwolffpottery.com

Campo de Fiori
1815 N. Main St.
Sheffield, MA 01257
campodefiori.com

Guy Wolff Pottery
1249 Bantam Rd.
Bantam, CT 06750
guywolff.com

Pergola
7 E. Shore Rd.
New Preston, CT 06777
pergolahome.com

Shakespeare's Garden
25 Obtuse Rd. S
Brookfield, CT 06804
shakespearesgarden.net

Snug Harbor Farm
87 Western Ave.
Kennebunk, ME 04043
snugharborfarm.com

Winston Flowers
Locations in and near Boston plus a
Greenwich, CT, location
winstonflowers.com

SOIL

Fafard Organic Potting Soil
fafard.com

Logee's Greenhouses
141 North St.
Danielson, CT 06239
logees.com

McEnroe Organic Farm
194 Coleman Station Rd.
Millerton, NY 12546
mcenroeorganicfarm.com

Organic Mechanic
organicmechanicsoil.com

DESIGN

Andrea Filippone
ajfdesign.com

ACKNOWLEDGMENTS

This book was born when James Baggett asked if I would be willing to write an article on indestructible houseplants for *Country Gardens* magazine. "Sure," I said, and the list of worthies to fill that story kept expanding. Tom Fischer took it from there. He wondered if I would be willing to write another book about houseplants—indestructible ones. But you also made it happen. You called in to radio shows and asked me for bulletproof recommendations. You went to my Facebook page (plantswisebytovahmartin) and sought suggestions. I thank you all for your input.

I thank my friends and fellow indestructible houseplant enthusiasts who generously shared their collections and knowledge. Andrea Filippone, Lee Link, Michael Trapp, Marianne Vandenburgh, and David Whitman and Peter Stiglin of Pergola all made this book special, and they proved I'm not the only one who goes nuts collecting plants.

I also thank my friends Dennis Sega and Rob Girard, who always miraculously appear every time I need to lift a heavy plant, move some furniture, or drill a hole in a pot. As always, Peter Wooster has been a role model. I honestly don't know where I'd be without my friends. And I'd better not forget Einstein, my trusty research assistant, who did the bounce and stress testing.

Most important, this book would be nowhere without Kindra Clineff. Her support, insight, creativity, feedback, expertise with the camera, and warm friendship made this book come together visually. She is brilliant, and heaven to work with. And Kindra has a support team behind her to thank—especially her partner, Tim Preston, and her sister, Jody Clineff, who helped pull the liaison together.

So many other people have influenced me over the years, especially my mother-in-law, Joy Logee Martin. Joy taught me everything I know. But these mentors are just the tip of the iceberg. You've heard it said that nothing can be accomplished without getting a village behind you. Well, the whole plant community has inspired me. This book is just one fruit of many that grew as a result.

A

B

TOVAH MARTIN emerged from twenty-five years working at Logee's Greenhouses with a serious houseplant addiction. Author of the classics *The Unexpected Houseplant*, *The New Terrarium*, and *Tasha Tudor's Garden*, Tovah has written more than a dozen gardening books. She served as garden editor for *Victoria* magazine throughout its lifetime and was named the new *Victoria*'s Writer in Residence for 2012. In addition, her articles appear in a broad range of magazines and periodicals, including *Country Gardens*, *Garden Design*, *Coastal Home*, *Martha Stewart Living*, *Traditional Home*, *Design New England*, *Yankee*, *The Litchfield County Times*, and *The Daily Telegraph*. For two years she served as segment producer and frequent guest on the PBS television series *Cultivating Life*, and she is a repeat guest on the CBS *Sunday Early Show*. Tovah teaches houseplant cultivation to Master Gardeners and lectures extensively throughout the country.

An accredited Organic Land Care Professional through NOFA, Tovah gardens fanatically and organically both indoors and throughout her seven-acre Connecticut garden. In addition to bestowing their Sarah Chapman Francis Medal for outstanding literary achievement on Tovah in 2008, The Garden Club of America and the Litchfield Garden Club awarded her honorary memberships. *People, Places, Plants* magazine called her "one of the top 10 most influential educators in gardening" and the Massachusetts Horticultural Society honored her with its Gold Medal "for extraordinary service to horticulture, especially greenhouses and indoor plants." For those who might need more hand-holding with their houseplants, Tovah provides advice and troubleshooting via her blog at plantswise.com. Join her on Facebook at plantswisebytovahmartin.

KINDRA CLINEFF

KINDRA CLINEFF travels far and wide specializing in location photography for commercial and editorial clients. She regularly produces feature assignments for national magazines, and her images have appeared in numerous books. Kindra also collaborated with Tovah Martin on her recent books, *The Unexpected Houseplant* and *The New Terrarium*. When not chasing light, Kindra can be found cultivating heirloom vegetables and attempting to tame the perennial garden of her seventeenth-century home in Essex County, Massachusetts.

TOVAH MARTIN